100 Country Houses

KT-226-445

100 Country Houses

NEW RURAL ARCHITECTURE

edited by Beth Browne

images
Publishing

Published in Australia in 2009 by
The Images Publishing Group Pty Ltd
ABN 89 059 734 431
6 Bastow Place, Mulgrave, Victoria 3170, Australia
Tel: +61 3 9561 5544 Fax: +61 3 9561 4860
books@imagespublishing.com
www.imagespublishing.com

Copyright © The Images Publishing Group Pty Ltd 2009
The Images Publishing Group Reference Number: 821

All rights reserved. Apart from any fair dealing for the purposes of private study, research, criticism or review as permitted under the Copyright Act, no part of this publication may be reproduced, stored in a retrieval system or transmitted in any form by any means, electronic, mechanical, photocopying, recording or otherwise, without the written permission of the publisher.

National Library of Australia Cataloguing-in-Publication entry:

Title:	100 country houses : new rural architecture / editor: Beth Browne.
ISBN:	9781864703320 (hbk.)
Subjects:	Country homes.
	Architecture, Domestic.
Dewey Number:	728.6

Edited by Beth Browne

Production by The Graphic Image Studio Pty Ltd, Mulgrave, Australia
www.tgis.com.au

Pre-publishing services by Splitting Image Colour Studio Pty Ltd, Australia

Printed on 150gsm HannoArt silk matt by Everbest Printing Co. Ltd., in Hong Kong/China

IMAGES has included on its website a page for special notices in relation to this and its other publications. Please visit www.imagespublishing.com.

CONTENTS

CONTENTS (continued)

CONTENTS (continued)

PREFACE

BETH BROWNE

EDITOR

The 100 contemporary country homes featured in the following pages range from traditional (with a twist) to highly experimental and their sheer diversity challenges any preconceived ideas regarding a quintessential country house. Each project exemplifies the shift towards forward-thinking design, which focuses on sustainability and actively engages in a responsive and responsible relationship with the land. These selected projects are from locations as diverse as Iceland, the Czech Republic, Germany, New Zealand, Canada, Switzerland, Mexico, Italy, Japan, Sweden, Greece, the UK, Slovenia, Spain, the USA and Australia. Together they encourage a broader understanding of what 'country house' means to people in different parts of the world, in places where space is sometimes more but often less readily available.

The effects of climate change are becoming increasingly apparent to those who live in remote areas, where lakes and dams long relied on for water supply and recreation are rapidly drying or where flash floods and snowstorms are devastating crops and livestock. It is no surprise therefore that environmentally sensitive, low-impact architecture is becoming the norm for new rural homes. Hydronic heating, photovoltaic arrays and solar panels, cross ventilation and rainwater collection are becoming almost requisite elements in new building generally, but it is arguably more incumbent upon those who design and own houses on large tracts of land in areas that are constantly subject to the forces of nature to harness this abundant natural energy supply and significantly reduce their impact on the environment.

Rural and remote areas around the world encompass a vast array of climates and site conditions. The houses in this book are sited on pastureland and mountains, beside lakes and vineyards, and in woodlands, rainforests and coastal regions. Many of the architects faced a combination of challenging site conditions including steep slopes, high fire danger, landslip or landslide zones, falling trees, high winds and even seismic activity. Some of these houses were designed to withstand frost, snow, extreme heat and bushfires – all in a single year. Of course, these challenges also come with their own unique opportunities for dramatic views, absolute privacy and a connection with nature that is simply unattainable in cities and sprawling suburbs.

The following houses all represent a common aspiration to live within the landscape rather than just admire it from afar. In many instances, this connection with the environment is subtly created by visually linking structural lines to those naturally occurring on the site, or by utilising local stone, timber and earth as construction materials so that the house blends seamlessly with its surroundings and evolves in response to the landscape. Turf roofs are employed to provide topographical continuity and help to conceal buildings when viewed from higher elevations. Even given the ample space available in remote areas, many of these houses incorporate enclosed courtyard areas for protection from wind, fast-changing weather and insects. These courtyards and terraces also serve to maximise passive solar gain and promote cross ventilation. Another common design theme is the use of multiple, adaptable zones, which afford a flexibility of space that can be opened up or closed off according to need.

This collection of 100 of the world's best rural and remote houses was a pleasure to research and is testament to the talent and creativity of the architects and photographers who have kindly allowed us to publish their work. We hope you enjoy discovering the work of these architects as much as we have enjoyed compiling this book.

19TH-CENTURY FARMHOUSE

ERIN, ONTARIO, CANADA

SCOTT MORRIS ARCHITECTS

This 110-year-old, 240-square-metre original Victorian farmhouse underwent an addition and renovation that increased its size to 410 square metres. It is now a fully accessible home for an active family of four living 21st-century lifestyles.

The addition addresses specific needs while maintaining the integrity and style of the existing house. The design features of the addition are consistent with the original architectural features, making a seamless transition.

Rising to the challenge of making this country house wheelchair accessible meant approaching the house with a fresh perspective. The new floor plan allows for a barrier-free zone allowing maximum independence in a beautiful environment with no resemblance to institutional spaces.

Porch and roof patterns are repeated, the addition is gabled and the chimneys are kept in line along the rooftop, in keeping with the home's original style. After that, it was just a matter of paying attention to the details. The exterior brickwork, windows and gingerbread trim as well as interior floor finishes, paint colours and door and window trims all match the originals. The bedroom wings are extra large for ease of wheelchair movement and a caregiver's presence without the feeling of being crowded. The plan also incorporates a huge media room with fireplace and ample floor space for entertaining and relaxing.

New landscaped gardens and gently sloping bricked pathways provide easy access to a house that promotes independent living within a beautifully restored and maintained traditional setting.

1

2

5

3

4

1   Front view: original house and addition
2   Back view: addition and original house
3   Living room
4   Den
5   View from new deck behind garage

Photography: Philip Castleton

5 BEECH LANE
KINGSCLIFF, NEW SOUTH WALES, AUSTRALIA

SCOTT CARPENTER ARCHITECT

A white rendered 'concrete' box floating over a polished charcoal block base and anchored centrally by a glass breezeway, 5 Beech Lane is quintessential casual living with a solid dose of bold minimalism.

The house is set on expansive landscaped gardens and flanked by water. Reed ponds lie along the southern entry boardwalk and a 20-metre infinity-edge lap pool stretches the entire length of northern boundary.

The house is divided into two pavilions: the sleeping box at the lane end and the entertainment box towards the beach. The plan then separates into four distinct zones: a guest bedroom wing and guest entertainment area on the ground floor and private bedrooms and private living spaces on the upper level.

The hub of the home is the breezeway. It is open to the north but protected from the elements by a shielded glazed roof and a combination of timber battens and fixed-glass louvres. It simultaneously links and separates the four zones, acting as the central circulation zone and 'airlock'. The line between indoors and outdoors is subtly blurred as doors disappear behind walls and decks continue inside. Although the aesthetic may suggest otherwise, the vast majority of the structure is lightweight timber framing, chosen because it is appropriately low in embodied energy.

While state-of the-art technology has been utilised extensively, the design is driven by strict ESD principles. All rooms are oriented to the north and protected on the north, east and west by a combination of generous eaves and automatic external roll-down blinds. External and internal louvres allow for thorough cross-ventilation in all rooms.

Stormwater is collected, stored and reused for the toilet, laundry, pool and garden. Any overflow is stored in a filtration tank and slowly dispersed into the sand rather than entering the street stormwater system.

2

1 Entry
2 Light pond
3 Reed pond
4 Bedroom
5 Garage
6 Lap pool
7 Spa
8 Breezeway
9 Guest entertainment
10 Alfresco dining
11 Kitchenette
12 Storage/services
13 Bathroom
14 Laundry
15 Drying yard
16 Deck
17 Dressing room
18 Master bedroom
19 Living
20 Meals
21 Kitchen
22 Fireplace
23 Void
24 Bar
25 Theatre
26 Cellar
27 Pump room
28 Surfboard store

4

3

5

3 The house is set among reed ponds and extensive landscaped gardens

4 Floor plan

5 Walls disappear as the alfresco dining deck is brought inside

6 The basement wine bar and cellar

7 The breezeway is the central circulation core and the 'lungs' of the home

8 The casual guest entertaining area

Photography: Brian Usher - Creative Jungle (2-7); Brent Middleton (8)

9 POINT HOUSE

DANDENONG RANGES, VICTORIA, AUSTRALIA

ITN ARCHITECTS

This small family house of 135 square metres is located in the Dandenong Ranges, a low mountain range east of Melbourne. The land is accompanied by a 'perfect storm' of issues: the 1.6-hectare site is very steep, dropping 50 metres across its length, and in a high fire danger and high landslip zone. The site is also covered by towering mountain ash trees, making access and construction a real challenge.

These particular conditions inspired a design influenced by aspects of the early Case Study houses of California. The landslip issues and potential for falling trees led to the use of an all-steel frame. As the site is on the south side of the mountain, and in shade for a lot of the year, the glazing was maximised to capture the rare sun and the spectacular views of Melbourne below. It was necessary to minimise the amount of potentially very expensive landslip-resistant footings required by having only nine points of contact, with much of the building and outdoor living space cantilevered over the circular drive required for fire access.

The small, perfectly square upper plan maximised the building's volume and minimised the more costly exterior surface area in order to work with the structural system and budget. The house is clad in Colorbond steel for economy, ease of maintenance and good fire performance. The design also allows for extra rooms to be hung below the structure without additional footings. The detailing and finishes were kept as simple as possible to allow the house to act as an unobtrusive frame to the dramatic 360-degree forest views. The house has since been struck by lightning and one falling tree, but is still going strong.

1   View from southeast corner of house
2   View from corner of deck to living room
3   Upper floor plan
4   Lower floor plan

3

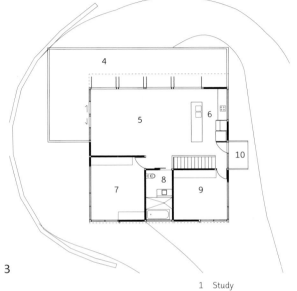

1   Study
2   Bathroom
3   Laundry
4   Deck
5   Living
6   Kitchen
7   Bedroom 1
8   Bathroom
9   Bedroom 2
10 Entry

0   5m

1

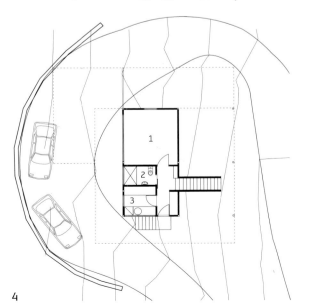

2

4

5

6

5   Bedroom 1
6   Living room
7   View to bathroom and bedroom 1
8   Bathroom
9   View from study at sunset

Photography: Aidan Halloran

ACTON HOUSE

ACTON PARK, TASMANIA, AUSTRALIA

PRESTON LANE ARCHITECTS PTY LTD WITH INTERIA

Acton House is located on the northern edge of a broadacre rural property in the heart of Acton Park, Tasmania. A row of pine trees lines the northern boundary, with access to the site via a long driveway from the south. The project brief was to provide a contemporary residence free from clutter and offering a clear separation between the public and private spaces of the house. As a result the plan is composed of two pavilions: one for living and one for sleeping.

The house has been sited to maximise views over the property's rural setting, while making use of existing vegetation on the site to conceal neighbouring properties. Its orientation aligns with the row of pine trees, and terminates with the broad landscape view to the east.

Stretching out into the landscape, a stack bond concrete block wall defines the entry to the house. A row of trees was planted on this axis to help further delineate the entry. When these trees mature they will also conceal an existing kennel building on the site. On approach to the front door, timber decking aligns with the concrete wall and continues into the house, through a window and out the other side, enhancing the connection to the outside.

Masonry walls flank both pavilions in an east–west direction, setting up a dialogue with the row of pine trees and providing a sense of containment from within. The pavilions are connected by a gallery/study area adjacent to the entry. A deck and courtyard space are located on either side of this gallery, providing external areas that are sheltered from the wind at different times of the day. These spaces also provide the owners with privacy from a riding trail that circles the property.

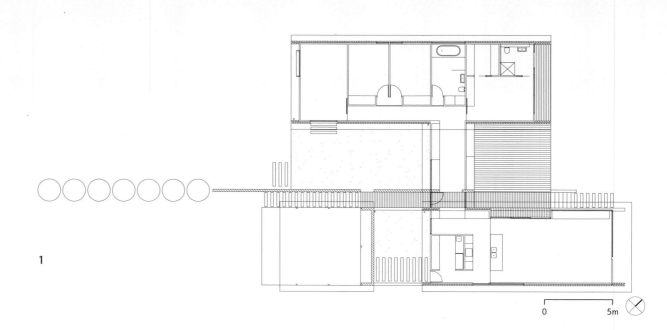

1

0   5m

1   Floor plan
2   Northern elevation

2

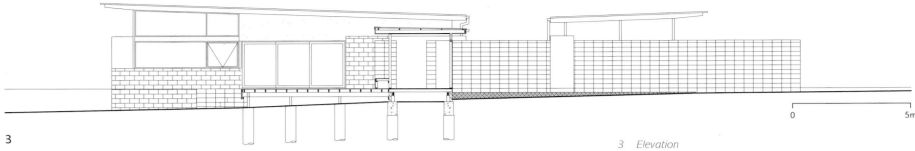

3

3   Elevation
4   Front entry
5   Private deck space
6   View of the living space
7   View of the kitchen
8   Gallery space with concealed study

Photography: Jonathan Wherrett

0   5m

4

5

6

7

8

AHIKOUKA WEEKEND RETREAT

WAIRARAPA, NEW ZEALAND

NOVAK+MIDDLETON ARCHITECTS LIMITED

Located in an old apple orchard in the rural district of Wairarapa in the southern region of New Zealand's North Island, the Ahikouka Weekend Retreat was conceived as a series of apple boxes sitting lightly on the land. The intention was to reinterpret the New Zealand building tradition, the crafting of timber and the expression of structure, cladding, lining and joinery in a raw and unique way.

The building consists of two simple boxes oriented on the primary axis of the site and linked by an external gallery. The boxes have been positioned on the site to maximise the visual expanse, while using the eastern shelter belt to create a sense of enclosure. The structure of the boxes has a logical and coherent rhythm reminiscent of apple packing cases stacked and ready for transport. The building skin alludes to its internal functions, utilising transparency for the living zones and solidity in the private spaces.

The entry is intentionally understated, opening to a large interconnected open-plan living area, positioned centrally to provide spaces where various family holiday functions can occur independently but remain connected. Bedroom spaces have been positioned at each end of the building and are more discrete than the living spaces to provide sheltered and restful areas, removed from the interactive living environment. Long slot windows have been positioned adjacent to bunk beds to provide individual control of view, sun and aspect. The living spaces open on both sides to the outside and the sun, analogous to a tent, while the bunkrooms remain enclosed and cool.

The unadorned natural timber façade provides a connection to nature and is set to weather in its rural environment. The concept incorporates simple sustainable design principles of water collection, 'wetback' water heating, waste management, double glazing and material selection.

The strong uncomplicated solid form with its inserted expanse of glass heightens the experience of the site, affording the feeling of being close to, but protected from, the elements. This creates a sense of shelter in close connection with the environment and provides a setting that captures the essential spirit of the New Zealand holiday retreat.

1

2

1 Boardwalk
2 Bunk room
3 Bathroom
4 Utility
5 Kitchen
6 Dining/living
7 Bedroom
8 Dressing room
9 Garage
10 Store/plant room
11 Terrace
12 Deck
13 Driveway
14 Future pool

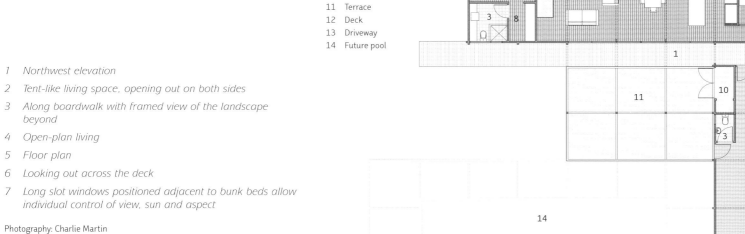

1 Northwest elevation
2 Tent-like living space, opening out on both sides
3 Along boardwalk with framed view of the landscape beyond
4 Open-plan living
5 Floor plan
6 Looking out across the deck
7 Long slot windows positioned adjacent to bunk beds allow individual control of view, sun and aspect

Photography: Charlie Martin

5

3

4

6

7

AMILEKA

BYRON BAY HINTERLAND, NEW SOUTH WALES,
AUSTRALIA

SHARON FRASER ARCHITECTS PTY LTD

Amileka is set on a flat site with spectacular sweeping views to the west. The site's existing trees are concentrated at the perimeter, except for one large, stand-alone, 100-year-old cudgeree tree. This tree became a design focus: it frames and adds another layer to the western view. The single-storey house is U-shaped in plan, balancing a western view with a northern aspect to take advantage of the terrific views to the west yet remain protected from the harsh western sun in summer.

The owners wanted to be able to 'step off' the house on all sides without being perched above the land, as so often happens with heavily contoured sites. They also wanted a choice of living and entertaining areas to provide flexibility at different times of the day depending on the season, weather and the number of people using the space. An alternative 'introverted' or 'quiet' outdoor space (the central eastern courtyard) was included to provide respite from the 'outside' context of the site and from prevailing winds.

The house operates as a flexible machine, according to the time of day, temperature or season, by means of movable and operable elements such as sliding walls, enormous doors (up to 6.5 metres long), retractable shade/insect screens and mechanically operated pergola elements. Outdoor and indoor living spaces were to have equal importance. The house can be completely opened up, so that inside and outside areas connect seamlessly.

As the entire floor is a concrete slab, most of it polished and exposed, the architect decided to insulate and heat it using a hydronic system that is solar heated and gas boosted (rather than electric). Photovoltaic cells (for electricity) and solar panels (to heat water) have been installed and the house also incorporates good cross ventilation and major rainwater collection (with no town water connection). The design allows for sun in winter, but the brutal western summer sun is screened by retractable shades in summer.

Although the main entertaining terrace is quite deep, the impact of natural light in the adjacent room is minimised by the mechanical adjustable pergola. The terrace can be an outdoor room when the pergola blades are open, or fully covered on a rainy day. The aim was not to blend or camouflage the house in its context, but rather to insert a clean modern building within the setting.

This project won the Australian Institute of Architects NSW Country Division 2008 Architecture Award.

1   West outdoor terrace

2   Northwest corner of house (living room, west outdoor terrace) with glass pool fence in foreground; rabbit sculpture by Melbourne sculptor Peter McLisky

3   Looking from north, inside pool enclosure

4   Northwest corner of house: pool, daybed and pergola in foreground

1

3

4

2

1	Entry
2	Pool
3	Pump room
4	Ensuite
5	Terrace
6	Bedroom
7	Pantry
8	Kitchen
9	Living
10	Fire pit
11	Wardrobe
12	Store
13	Laundry
14	Dry courtyard
15	Bathroom
16	East courtyard
17	Study
18	Garage
19	North lawn
20	West outdoor terrace
21	Firewood store

7

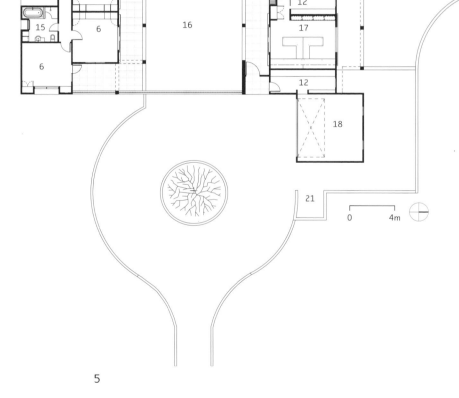

5

6

5 Floor plan

6 Living room featuring sunken lounge in foreground, sliding gantry panel concealing shelving on left and fireplace on right with painting that slides up into ceiling to reveal TV

7 Sunken lounge, shelving and sliding gantry panel behind

8 West façade of house, pool in foreground

9 View from west outdoor terrace towards living space, kitchen in foreground

10 Looking from master bedroom towards west outdoor terrace, rabbit sculpture in background

Photography: Richard Powers

BALLANDEAN HOUSE

BALLANDEAN, QUEENSLAND, AUSTRALIA

ARKHEFIELD

The Tobin Winery is located on a north-facing, gently sloping site on a vineyard in the heart of the Granite Belt of southeast Queensland. The vineyard merges with remnant scrub that borders a creek, while occasional protrusions of local granite punctuate the landscape. The house is located at the top of the site, looking down over the vines, road and creek towards the distant hills.

The concept for the overall form originated as a response to the landscape – primarily the linearity of the vines and the layered nature of the topography. The roof is folded down at both ends, referencing the Australian shed and celebrating the notion of shelter. The strength and solidity of the helmet roof is a response to the harsh climate and rugged landscape. As opposed to touching the earth lightly, the solid form grounds itself and creates a sense of stability and resilience. Services are relegated to the lower black boxes, with living and sleeping spaces enjoying the soft southern light filtering through the roof skylight that manifests as a lantern and entry marker at night.

The poles, water tanks, awnings and pool employ a 'homestead' strategy to define the external rooms. In time the surrounding vegetation will grow and ancillary structures will evolve to breathe life into the interstitial spaces.

Deliberately avoiding a light, feathered, timber-and-tin structure, Arkhefield has created a solid, grounded form that offers protection from the often-harsh weather. At the same time, the view of the vineyard is beautifully captured.

1   *East elevation showing the wrap of the roofing element*
2   *Northwest view of the house over the vineyard*
3   *Southern view of the house showing the garden and bluegum poles that will support the vines*

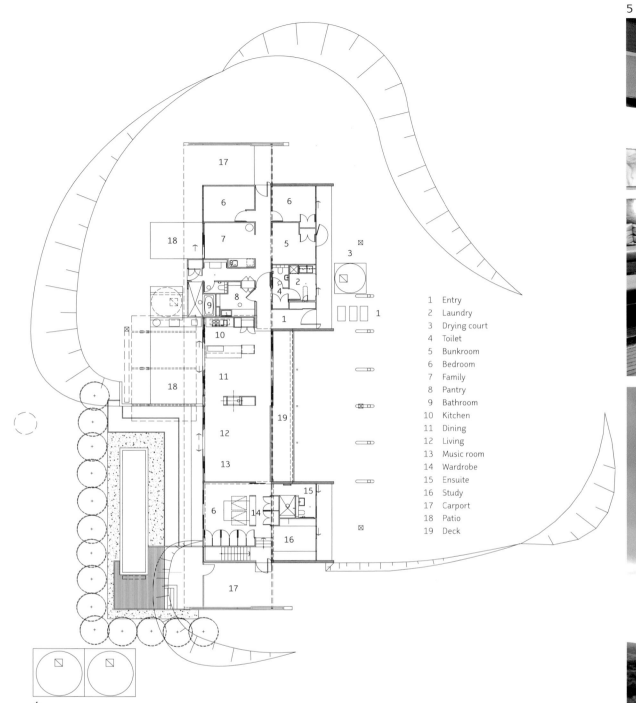

1 Entry
2 Laundry
3 Drying court
4 Toilet
5 Bunkroom
6 Bedroom
7 Family
8 Pantry
9 Bathroom
10 Kitchen
11 Dining
12 Living
13 Music room
14 Wardrobe
15 Ensuite
16 Study
17 Carport
18 Patio
19 Deck

4   Ground floor plan
5   The elevated lap pool runs half the house's length
    along the north elevation
6   Entry and the south garden beyond
7   Interior view of the one-room-deep living space allowing
    for optimal ventilation and visual access to the environment
8   The outdoor verandah to the north takes centre stage
    and provides access to the lap pool

Photography: Scott Burrows, Aperture Architectural Photography

6

7

BENDEMEER HOUSE

LAKE HAYES, QUEENSTOWN, NEW ZEALAND

WARREN AND MAHONEY

The house takes its cues from the forms and materials explored initially by the architects at the Bendemeer woolshed and pavilion, and from Warren and Mahoney's earlier Amisfield Wine Company cellar door building nearby on Lake Hayes Road. Natural stone, steel and timber cladding in a regionalist style has been explored and detailed in a contemporary manner.

The 590-square-metre house is separated into five stand-alone stone and timber 'sheds' grouped around a walled entry courtyard, each with a 45-degree gabled roof in the manner of Miles Warren's quintessential Canterbury houses of the 1960s. These separate but connected pavilions allow the house to remain legibly scaled in the landscape, and also to adjust itself to suit its occupants – intimate for a couple and expanding to suit a wider group as required.

A great room centre pavilion is flanked by the main bedroom and garaging to the east, with guest bedrooms and a guest apartment symmetrically aligned at the west. A glazed gallery links the otherwise freestanding structures and a reflecting pool and outdoor fireplace are arranged to the north.

Materials in their natural state (steel, timber, stone and concrete) predominate, both inside and out. No plasterboard has been used in the interior linings. The house is intended as an antidote to the urban house experience and its design aspirations on behalf of the client are anti-urban, anti-artifice.

An arabesque laser-cut metal screen over the plastered entry wall and extendable sunshading within the northern steel frames will soon be completed.

1   View of house in landscape from northeast
2   Outdoor terrace and reflecting pool to north
3   Entry to great room

1

2

3

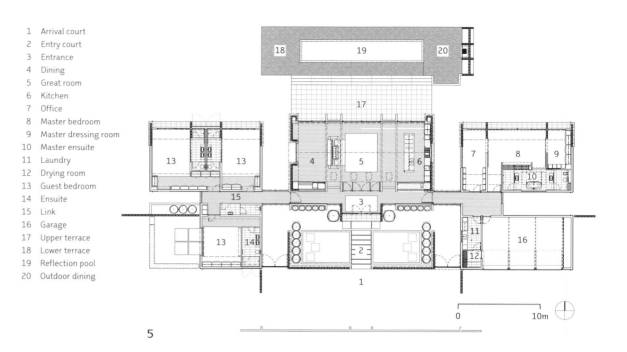

1   Arrival court
2   Entry court
3   Entrance
4   Dining
5   Great room
6   Kitchen
7   Office
8   Master bedroom
9   Master dressing room
10 Master ensuite
11 Laundry
12 Drying room
13 Guest bedroom
14 Ensuite
15 Link
16 Garage
17 Upper terrace
18 Lower terrace
19 Reflection pool
20 Outdoor dining

5

4

4 Great room

5 Floor plan

6 Entry to great room – pivot doors for summer/winter use

7 Library/office links to master bedroom

8 Kitchen

9 Master bathroom

Photography: Stephen Goodenough

BLACK HOUSE

VALLE DE BRAVO, MEXICO

BGP ARQUITECTURA

A magnificent view is the main feature of this retreat located on the hill of a small village 150 kilometres from Mexico City. The house is sited under a canopy within the landscape with as few interior elements as possible.

Black House is also one-half terrace, protected from the exterior conditions when necessary by means of 4-metre-tall sliding glass panels on the landscape side and a wall as high as the garage doors on the village side. The exposed concrete canopy emphasises views and meets the criteria of the local building code, which calls for typical construction elements and materials such as pitched roofs and Spanish tile. The house is oriented towards the south, optimising the views and blocking sun in summer but not in winter. Like the roof, the solid block is all exposed concrete on the inside and marble on the outside with slots carefully placed to allow glances through to the surroundings.

The rest of the site retains the natural slope and local, highly adaptive vegetation frames the view and wraps around the family's vegetable garden. The covered roof garden is also an important area for outdoor living. Interior materials flow out into exterior spaces and vice versa, blurring the line between inside and outside. Black House is the Mediterranean house revisited, allowing its inhabitants to live within the view rather than just looking at it.

1 Crystal box

2,3 View of the public area opened to the lake

1

2

3

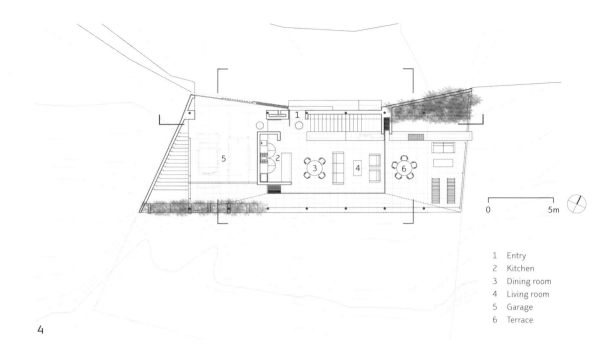

1 Entry
2 Kitchen
3 Dining room
4 Living room
5 Garage
6 Terrace

0   5m

6

7

4   Main floor plan

5   Façade from the lake

6   Entrance to the public area
    from the private area

7   Garage

8   Kitchen

Photography: Rafael Gamo

BLUMBERG/LYNN HOUSE

HUDSON RIVER VALLEY, NEW YORK, USA

ALFREDO DE VIDO

This house is located in the Hudson River Valley in New York, an area that combines the scenic beauty of farmed fields and wooded hillsides. The main design idea was to take full advantage of the views, which are striking in all seasons.

A long drive leads to the house. Setback requirements influenced its placement on the site, so the house sits downhill from the approach on the hillside. Knowing that the first glimpse of the house would be of its roof, the architect designed a roofscape with a variety of shapes and openings and clad it with a luminous metal skin. The design is defined by these roofs and columns. Beneath them, the building's series of wings descends into the hillside.

A landscaped, gently rising path leads to the main door at the front of the house. Inside there is a slightly inclined ramp on axis with the central stone fireplace that leads into the main space, which contains all the main rooms and is richly detailed in wood. Built-in furniture, storage and lighting simplify the interior décor and contribute to the overall aesthetic. Within this flowing space, windows are carefully placed to bring in light and provide splendid views.

Several terraces also enjoy these views and provide areas for outdoor living; some are sheltered spaces and some are open to sun and sky. Down the hill on the lowest part of the site is a swimming pool with an infinity edge that leads the onlooker's eye into the landscape beyond.

1

1	Bedroom 1
2	Bedroom 2
3	Study
4	Kitchen
5	Living room
6	Dining room
7	Bridge
8	Entrance
9	Library
10	Office
11	File storage
12	Bathroom

0   6m

2

1 Large roofs shelter outdoor seating areas

2 First floor plan

3 View of rooftop as encountered from driveway

4 The fireplace is a central feature

5 Kitchen detailed to fit with the design of the house

Photography: Todd Mason

4

5

3

BOWEN MOUNTAIN RESIDENCE

BOWEN MOUNTAIN, NEW SOUTH WALES, AUSTRALIA

CPLUSC DESIGN CONSTRUCT

This house is nestled in the dense bushland of Bowen Mountain, an elevated rural region adjoining the Blue Mountains National Park in New South Wales with views back to Sydney. The topography and natural spring water veins allow dense vegetation to flourish, with limited area on which to build.

Commissioned as a weekender, this simple yet unconventional pavilion grew to include extensive landscaping, a swimming pool, a pool house and sauna facilities once construction had begun. An existing slab hut with a corrugated steel roof was retained in the scheme, recognising the inherent qualities of the traditional construction methods and local materials.

The structural steel frame was welded onsite prior to shot blasting and finishing in a two-part epoxy coating. Both new and recycled Australian hardwoods were then used to frame the steel structure with Western red cedar doors and windows used extensively to complete the space. This fenestration also provides connection from inside to outside, cross-ventilation, views and spatial flexibility from season to season.

A simple courtyard with shaded walkway connects old and new buildings and also acts as the point of entry to the pavilion. Over 1.8 kilometres of decking and 28,000 stainless steel screws were used in the construction of the decking platforms that surround the pavilion and the pool, ensuring that the project will stand the test of time.

Roof forms and fenestration allow light and breezes to penetrate spaces year-round. Careful consideration was given to passive solar design allowing the occupants to attenuate the thermal environment of the spaces. Generous outdoor spaces have integrated a native fishpond with decks and terraces that respond to the topography. Outdoor cooking facilities connect with the swimming pool and pool house, concealing the 100,000-litre water tank below. A sauna, day bed and outdoor shower complement the pool house entertaining area.

Both water and sewage are collected and treated onsite with LPG bottles supplying fuel for cooking, hot water and heating needs. Renewable Australian materials with natural finishes were used predominantly in the project complemented by stains, oils and plywoods.

1   The bedroom suite is located above the living area, with a private terrace taking advantage of the panoramic views to the east

2   The courtyard utilises Australian hardwood decking and provides a dramatic entrance element with framed views to the surrounding bushland

3   Large sliding doors within the expressed steel structure allow the living spaces to spill out to the terraces and decks

4   The sunken lounge creates an intimate zone within the open-plan living, kitchen and dining area

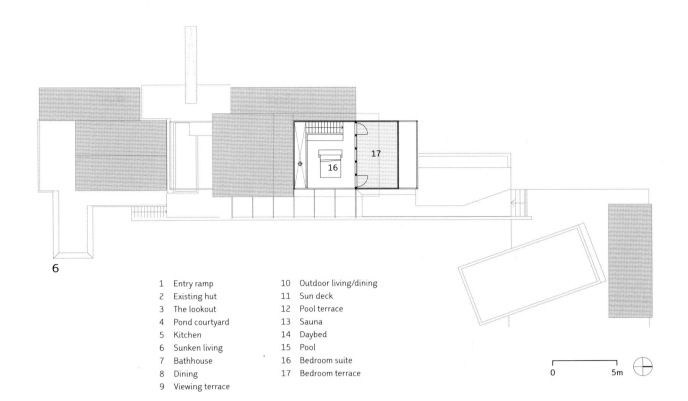

6

1 Entry ramp	10 Outdoor living/dining
2 Existing hut	11 Sun deck
3 The lookout	12 Pool terrace
4 Pond courtyard	13 Sauna
5 Kitchen	14 Daybed
6 Sunken living	15 Pool
7 Bathhouse	16 Bedroom suite
8 Dining	17 Bedroom terrace
9 Viewing terrace	

0   5m

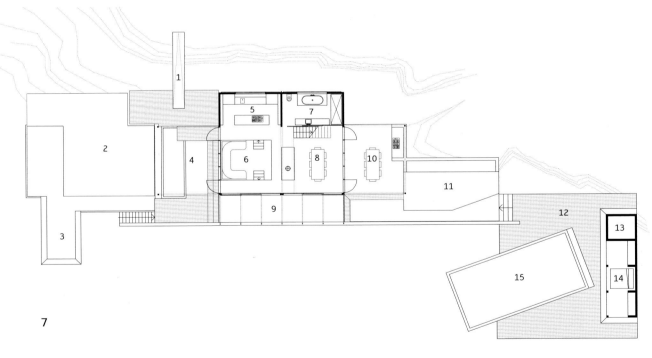

7

Opposite   *View from the existing hut towards the living pavilion;*
             extensive glazing creates a transparent structure
             filled with light and breeze

6   *First floor plan*

7   *Ground floor plan*

Photography: Murray Fredericks

BOWER HOUSE

GREAT OCEAN ROAD, VICTORIA, AUSTRALIA

FMD ARCHITECTS

This house contains individual zones for a couple and their two adult daughters, with opportunities for separate access to the different spaces. A large living and dining space with outdoor entertaining areas provides space to congregate with family members and friends. An important brief requirement was an area specifically for yoga practice that offers spatial isolation with an external outlook. The need for multiple flexible zones and spaces to allow for isolation and congregation was also a major consideration in the planning phase.

The curved path from the main living area to the main bedroom is an example of the influence of the owner's interest in yoga on the design. The external and internal walls between these spaces stretch themselves in three dimensions around the trees, which are a dominant feature of the site and had to be preserved. The presence of the trees is constant, yet their impact varies both internally and externally. The light they cast on and within the house creates a balanced relationship between the built form and nature, an effect that is continually evolving as the trees grow and the light changes with the seasons.

Opposite   Street view: the house embraces the trees

2   *View to the entry*

3   *Living room fireplace unit with main entry adjacent;
    the steel and stone elements stretch themselves to follow
    the building lines*

4   *Rear private courtyard*

5   *View from dining room to main bedroom*

6   *Floor plan*

7   *Living room and trees beyond*

8   *View of living room joinery and kitchen*

Photography: Shannon McGrath

3

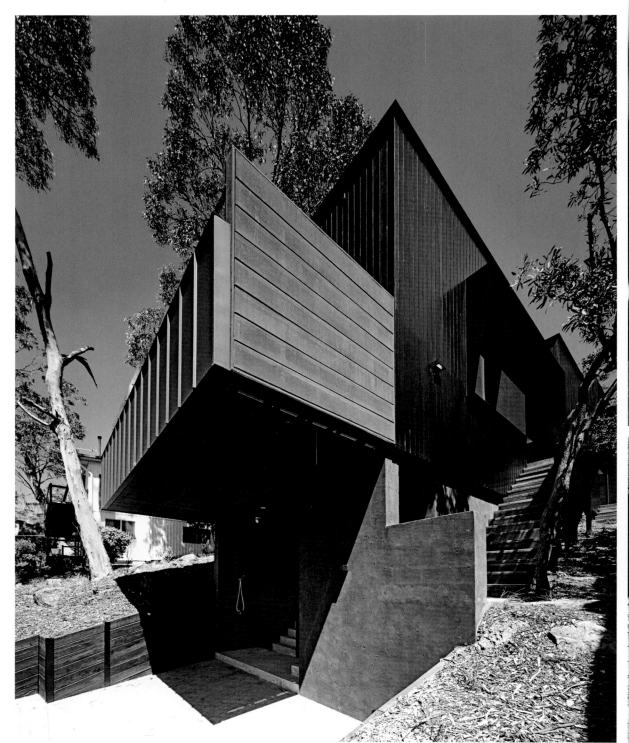

2

4

7

5

6

8

BRAMMELL RESIDENCE

OLD SNOWMASS, COLORADO, USA

STUDIO B ARCHITECTS

This 820-square-metre residence sits on a 3-hectare site on the fringe of a 730-hectare cattle ranch near the Elk Mountain Range in Old Snowmass, Colorado. The site's vegetation consists of sage, abundant wildflowers, scattered juniper trees and the occasional cactus.

The owners, originally from Tennessee, requested a contemporary interpretation of the ranch vernacular that is prevalent in the neighbouring valleys and surrounding ranchlands. The architect researched local agricultural structures and took many cues from these regional buildings in terms of massing, roof forms and exterior materials. The textures and colours of the materials evoke those of the landscape. Exterior materials include native limestone, reclaimed barn wood siding, aluminium siding, a cedar rain screen, vertical rusted steel panels and aluminium-clad windows and doors. The foundation system was specially engineered to accommodate the site's expansive soils.

The west elevation enjoys expansive pastoral views as well as vistas of distant alpine peaks, while the east side of the house revolves around a terraced courtyard for gatherings and is embraced by the uphill topography. The program is divided into a private wing, a public and service level and a guest area above the garage.

The Brammell Residence has won several American Institute of Architects design awards.

1   Main level plan
2   East elevation and context of the ranch landscape
3   Living room with native limestone fireplace
4   Perspective of the kitchen from the office
5   Guest bedroom with horizontal wood bed wall

Photography: Paul Warchol

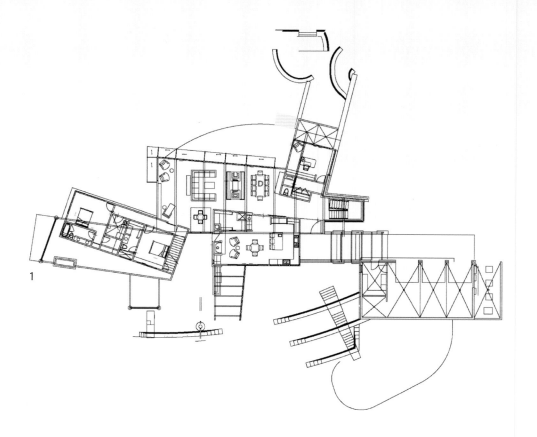

1

BREAM TAIL HOUSE

MANGAWHAI HEADS, NORTHLAND, NEW ZEALAND

SGA LTD (STRACHAN GROUP ARCHITECTS)

Located within a surveyed 1-hectare 'exclusive use' area, the Bream Tail House is a single level, low-slung building conceived as a bird-like form that has landed on the existing grassed and gravel terrace. The siting references the early Maori occupation of terraces, which is evident on the northeastern escarpment visible from the house. The core of the house straddles the existing 'modified' land by way of the existing gravel farm track to minimise the need to break up 'virgin' land. The roof folds down to the northeast, forming the 'head and beak', and the translucent rear 'tail' kicks up to catch the last of the afternoon light. Roof edges are 'frayed' with outrigged purlins and custom-made stainless steel gutters are used to feather out the roof edges. Weathered zinc roofing was chosen to reflect and merge with the colour of the sky.

The southern outdoor room and garage walls are heavier – stack-bonded half-height natural blockwork that has been clear finished to emulate the fractured layering of the sand and shells of the archaeological middens nearby. The garage and carport walls are partially excavated into the shaded toe of the northwest ridge. Water tanks are also excavated into this area behind the garage to prevent visual intrusion. Other walls are clad with black-stained, banded, textured plywood corresponding to the black-green of the puriri trees in shadow on the northwest ridge.

The joinery is either natural anodised aluminium or oiled cedar left to weather naturally. Banks of northeastern flap windows on gas struts open up the building like feathers 'breathing' and during occupancy give a sense of variation and movement of the building skin. Seaward and northeast terraces are formed in natural-finished cantilevered concrete to give a sense of lightness – they float up to 1 metre above the 18-metre terraced contour. Translucent and battened cedar upper walls to the rear of the house and carport area assist in 'lifting' the roof off the heavier concrete walls, as if raising the wings and tail from the body.

Opposite   Outdoor room

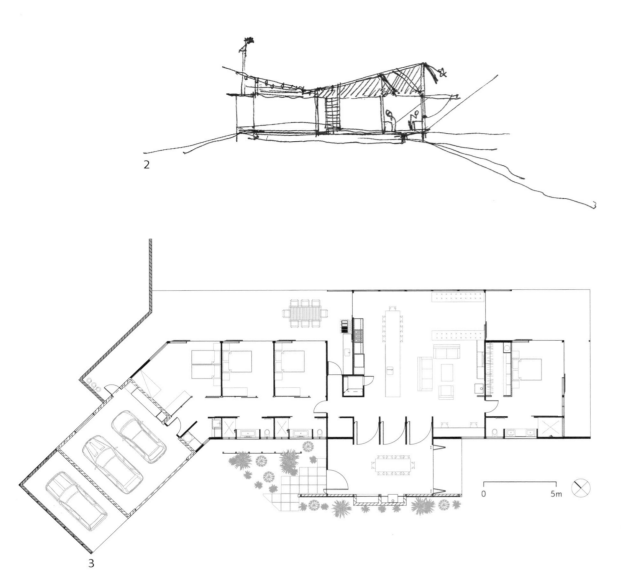

2

3

5

2 *Diagrammatic section*
3 *Floor plan*
4 *Northern façade*
5 *Dining area*
6 *Outdoor room*
7 *View from kitchen*
8 *Living area looking out to the Pacific Ocean and the Hen and Chickens Islands*

Photography: Patrick Reynolds

4

6

BUTEL PARK HOUSE

ARROWTOWN, NEAR QUEENSTOWN, NEW ZEALAND

CREATIVE ARCH

Set within stunning surroundings in Arrowtown, near Queenstown, this house enjoys the striking, rugged mountains of the Remarkables and Coronet Peak ski areas and majestic lakes as its backdrop. It was vital to capture such unrivalled views in the design of this truly wonderful home.

The owner's desire was for simplicity, but with deceptive depth and a very efficient house plan. The H shape of the four-bedroom plan creates well-designed zones, with the L-shaped living zone and the bedroom wing running the length of one leg. The plan allows for optimum flexibility, making it easy to rearrange furniture to suit a range of requirements, from an intimate dining setting through to a generous entertaining area. This home is an entertainer's dream, with a sumptuous kitchen that opens out to a flowing outdoor living space with a sheltered courtyard and back-to-back fireplace. With covenants to meet, Butel Park House is a familiar Queenstown building form – the steep pitched roofs and use of schist undoubtedly belong in the snow-capped mountain setting.

Robust materials, including a predominant use of insulated concrete panels, balance with a rhythmical use of glass openings and weatherboards to gable ends. The colours are subdued – earthy tones are used in conjunction with external timber and sleek timber cabinetry and flooring indoors to create a clean restful feel. This is a design that will truly stand the test of time in terms of style and durability – it is a lifestyle home that will withstand the rigours of its inhabitants living their lives to the fullest in this wondrous setting.

1   Floor plan
2   The approach
3   Informal living area with kitchen and formal living behind; views to an outdoor courtyard and fireplace complete the look and feel
4   The master bedroom captures the views

Photography: Henry Norcross

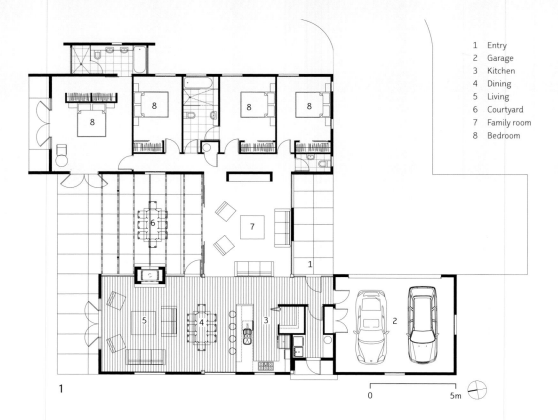

1   Entry
2   Garage
3   Kitchen
4   Dining
5   Living
6   Courtyard
7   Family room
8   Bedroom

1

0   5m

BYZANTINE HOUSE

AGHIA SOPHIA, MANI, GREECE

AIOLOU ARCHITECTS

Located within the southern Greek village of Aghia Sophia, parts of which date back to the 15th century, the Byzantine House enjoys stunning views both to the sea and up to the Taygetos Mountains that overlook the village from the east. Two stone walls were all that existed on this plot, the remnants of a house in the village. Amazingly, the entrance – with carved stone arch and key stones adorned with a mysterious sculptural relief of animals – had survived the ravages of time.

It was later discovered that the original phase of the house and part of the ruin were of Byzantine origin, dating back to the 17th century. A long planning procedure involving many negotiations with archaeological and building authorities led to a set of restrictions on how and what it was possible to build. The ruin and all materials found onsite had to be integrated into the design of the house, thus helping to tie the house to its local surroundings and create a unique home that respects and maintains a link to its past forms and materials. The footprint of the original building, dug into the local bedrock, also had to be maintained and thus determined the form and volume of the new building.

The main living spaces were retained upstairs and incorporated in an open-plan design allowing for the full view of the open roof and openings to all the featured views from around the room. The reclaimed floor was bought from a ruined church in Turkey and was probably originally a deck in a boat. The stairs begin in wood and change to stone at the lower level, where they meet the multiple-coat cement floor finish achieved by careful sanding, so that the different tones of each layer show

The exterior stone walls have been built using stones found onsite and new stone from the same quarry that the original material came from. They include bits of ceramics from the site, as did the original walls, and also the sculptural relief of animals around the entrances.

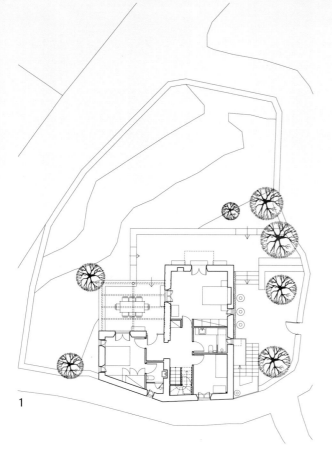

1

2

3

4

5

1   *Lower level floor plan*

2,3 *View of southwest façade*

4   *Upper-level living room*

5   *Central fireplace with built-in storage
       benches for firewood*

Photography: Kyriaki Dovinou and Lefteris Miaoulis
www.photothemata.gr

CAMOUFLAGE HOUSE

GREEN LAKE, WISCONSIN, USA

JOHNSEN SCHMALING ARCHITECTS

The Camouflage House sits on a steep lake bluff with its narrow, linear volume nestled into the hillside. Approaching the house from the rugged access road weaving through the site's heavily wooded plateau, the building's faint, low-slung silhouette virtually disappears in the surrounding vegetation. With its simple plan, restrained use of materials and precise detailing, the house achieves an elegant clarity and rustic warmth that avoids bucolic sentimentality.

The house's complex system of façade layers expresses an ambition to assimilate with its surroundings. Echoing the rhythmic shifts between the surrounding tree trunks, the building skin is composed of solids and voids. The first façade layer is clad in untreated vertical cedar and serves as a backdrop for a series of polychromatic Prodema wood veneer panels that reflect the hues of the surrounding deciduous trees. Over time, the cedar walls will weather to a silver-grey, while the wood veneer panels will retain their original colour and pristine finish.

From the small clearing of the entry court, the low roof of the open breezeway connecting the house and garage leads to a linear, glazed entry foyer that penetrates the two-storey, 250-square-metre building and terminates in a partially covered balcony with spectacular views of the lake. Stairs connect to the lower level, which is fully exposed on the lake side and houses all bedrooms, providing access to the zero-edge bluff terrace that stretches along the entire length of the building and to the master bedroom 'grotto', an intimate outdoor space between the western edge of the house and the site's imposing rock formation. On the upper level, kitchen, dining and living functions occupy an open space that can extend into the adjacent spacious screen porch by retracting the large, foldable glass door system. Throughout the spring, summer and autumn, the screen porch functions as the home's lung, taking advantage of the mild lake breezes.

Exposed integrally coloured concrete floors throughout the house complement the warmth of the MDF walls, as does a three-sided Corten steel-clad fireplace forming the focal point of the open living hall. Sustainable materials were used throughout the house, including low-VOC paints, recycled products, native woods and high-performance glazing.

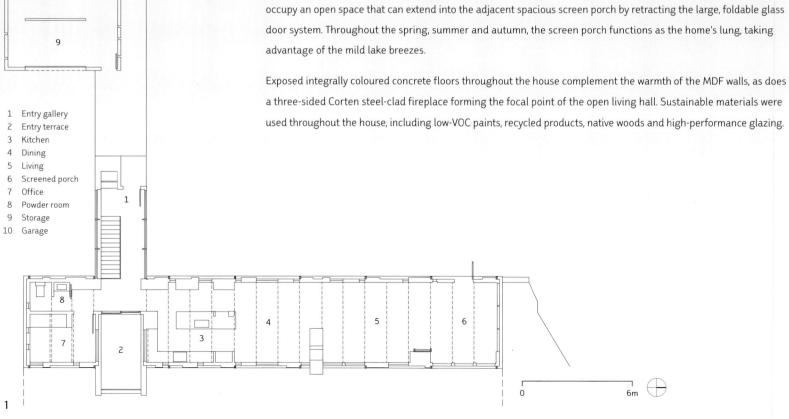

1   Entry gallery
2   Entry terrace
3   Kitchen
4   Dining
5   Living
6   Screened porch
7   Office
8   Powder room
9   Storage
10 Garage

2

5

6

3

1 *Floor plan*
2 *View of house from bluff*
3 *North view of house*
4 *Living hall from kitchen*
5 *Detail view of entry court façade*
6 *View of 'grotto' from bedroom*
7 *Dining room*

Photography: Kevin Miyazaki

4

7

CARABBIA HOUSE

TICINO, SWITZERLAND

DAVIDE MACULLO ARCHITETTO

Carabbia is a small village of approximately 600 inhabitants. It sits in a beautiful bowl on the western slope of Mount San Salvatore. The owner wished to live in an intimate space, as if in a shell. This 13- by 13-metre house offers privileged views of its beautiful surrounds, simultaneously providing a sense of protection and a sense of being projected into the landscape. Carved in a clear square geometry, the spaces meet the slope and extend in a spiral, fluent movement that constantly changes the inhabitant's perception of the interior space and its relation with the exterior.

The sloped roof follows the land's natural incline, presenting an organic rather than urban vernacular. Because the site slopes approximately 30 degrees facing west the volume was designed to adhere as closely as possible so that no earth was displaced from the construction site. The home's three main storeys are set on the site at shifted levels, providing a direct relationship to the outside from all parts of the house. Upon entering, the entire interior space and the related outdoor space become visible, enhancing perception of the house's volume. This relationship is continued throughout all parts of the building, making the outdoor space always part of the indoor experience and the volume appear larger than it actually is.

The functional areas are located on three main levels. An entrance mezzanine (with wardrobe storage) is set between the upper level (living) and the middle level (kitchen and dining), and the three bedrooms are located on the lower level. All levels are visually connected while maintaining their own characteristics.

This house was shortlisted for the WAN (World Architecture News) House of the Year in 2007.

Opposite   View from south

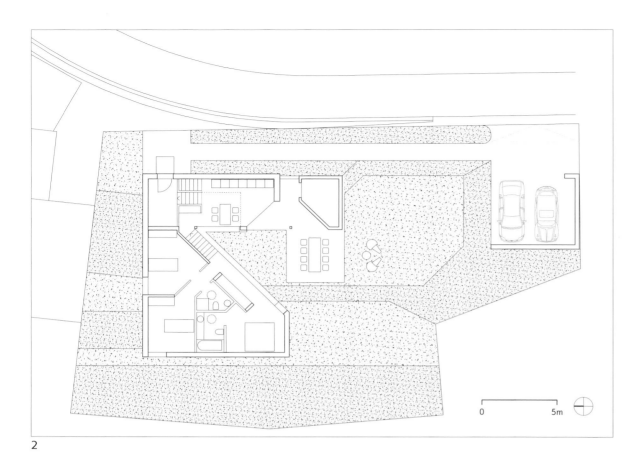

2

4

3

5

6

2 Floor plan
3 View to courtyard
4 Void over kitchen
5 Hall
6 Living room
7,8 Dining room

Photography: Pino Musi

7

8

CHURCH BAY HOUSE

CHURCH BAY, WAIHEKE ISLAND,
AUCKLAND, NEW ZEALAND

DANIEL MARSHALL ARCHITECT

The Church Bay House is a timeless four-bedroom family home with a strong connection to the surrounding landscape, maximising views across the vineyards to the many distant bays. The imagery presented in the clients' brief was a fusion of traditional Japanese and modern architecture. Use of natural materials was encouraged.

There were stringent planning regulations for the site - for example, the building was permitted to rise no more than 4 metres above the existing ground level. This helped drive the floor plan, with spaces arranged linearly along a loose axis and positioned towards the views. Because of the occasionally high winds, and in homage to Japanese dwelling forms, the house incorporates four courtyards with varying degrees of landscaping.

The functional nodes are laid out along a linear axis, separated by landscape elements and signified by differentiations in materiality and by sculptural echoes of the surrounding landscape forms.

1   Floor plan
2   View at sunset
3   Second living area (view from courtyard)
4   View from pool

Photography: Daniel Marshall

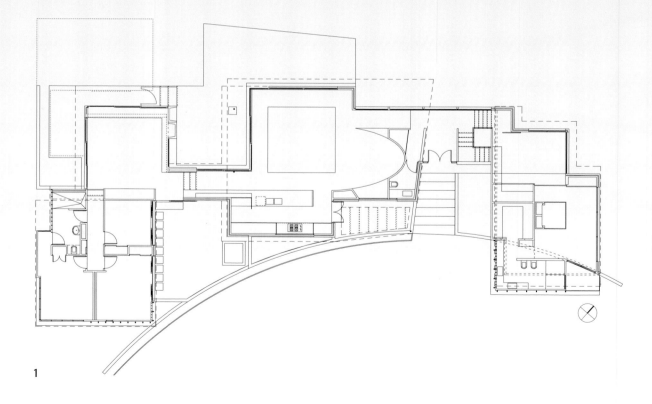

1

CLIFF HOUSE

ASPEN, COLORADO, USA

STUDIO B ARCHITECTS

This 930-square-metre residence is perched on a craggy rock outcropping overlooking both the Castle Creek River and the Elk Mountains. Previously, the large half-hectare site contained two older structures that were demolished and replaced with this house and its terraces, courts and gardens.

Several site conditions posed difficulties to the design process and construction. These included a natural rockslide path that required mitigation in the form of a rear rockfall barrier, bedrock that needed to be blasted to install the foundations, a division of program that required three differing mechanical systems and the intense climatic swings of winter and summer in Aspen. Along with these challenges, the site drops 7 metres across the footprint of the house, which required the house to step in plan accordingly.

The architecture is rooted in the angularity of the site's topography and is oriented to take advantage of both immediate and distant views. A bridge-like stairway links the public and private wings and a caretaker unit lies beneath the large garage/workshop area. The west elevation takes advantage of the sound of the river, the numerous mountain views and the ample sunshine found in Colorado. The entry side of the house opens onto a sculpture garden, reflecting pool and the morning sunlight.

The ambient sound and cooling effect of Castle Creek in the summer months played an integral role in how the rooms were arranged. The private master wing enjoys a view over the river and has a terrace with a spa. There are levels below both the master wing and the public zone with several bedrooms and playrooms for family and guests.

The material palette consists of composite wood siding, porcelain panels, metal roofing, board-formed concrete and aluminium doors and windows. Solar collecting panels heat the indoor pool and supplement the heating of the house.

1   The home clings to the edge with the river below
2   A low-profile roofline allows for views over the home

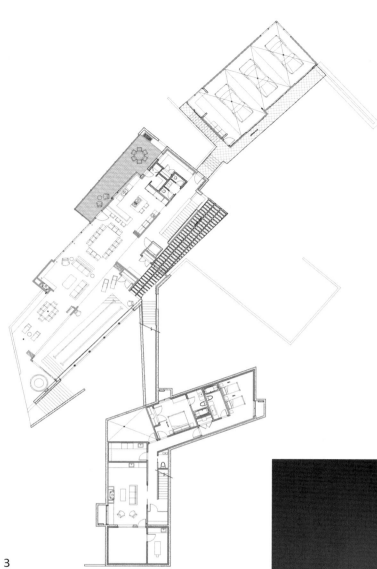

3   Main level floor plan

4   Pocket courtyards enjoy sun and views

5   Window placement allows views though the house

6   An open floor plan allows spaces to flow together

7   Large kitchen windows provide light and views

8   The stairway links the public to the private wings

Photography: Aspen Architectural Photography

THE CO$_2$ SAVER

LAKE LAKA, UPPER SILESIA, POLAND

PETER KUCZIA

Like a chameleon, this sustainable house blends with its surrounds on Lake Laka in Upper Silesia, Poland. Colourful planks in the timber façade reflect the tones of the landscape. The front window, clad in fibre cement, reveals and frames images of the countryside. Analogous to most living creatures, the building is symmetrical on the outside, although the internal zones are arranged asymmetrically according to function.

The built form is designed to optimise solar energy absorbtion. Approximately 80 percent of the building envelope faces south. The single-storey living space on the ground floor is externally clad with untreated larch boarding. Solar energy is gained via the set-in glazed patio. Solar collection panels are located on the roof and a photovoltaic system is planned for the future. The sun warms the dark façade of the 'black box' – a three-storey structure clad with charcoal-coloured fibre cement panels that reduces heat loss to the environment. A ventilation plant with a thermal recovery system enhances the passive and active solar energy concepts and offers a high standard of thermal insulation.

The design of the project was determined by the twin goals of low lifecycle costs and a reduction in construction costs. All details are simple, but well thought out. The house cost no more to construct than a conventional Polish house. Cost savings were made by the application of traditional building techniques and the use of local materials and recycled building elements.

The CO$_2$ Saver house won first prize for Best Silesian Architecture (Poland) in the Union of Polish Architects' competition and first prize for Best Façade in the Eternit competition (Germany). It was also nominated for other renowned worldwide competitions including the House of the Year Award (United Kingdom), the Zumtobel Group Award (Germany) and the European Mies van der Rohe Award (Spain).

1	Living room	10	Terrace
2	Dining room	11	Studio
3	Kitchen	12	Gallery
4	Storage	13	Patio
5	Porch	14	Room with view onto lake
6	Wardrobe	15	Corridor
7	Laundry	16	Bathroom
8	Bathroom	17	Green roof
9	Bedroom		

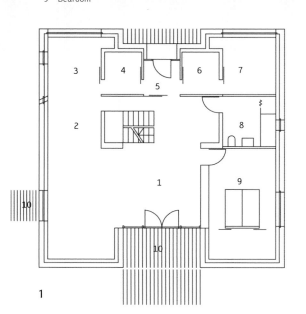

1

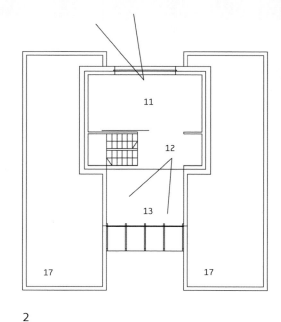

2

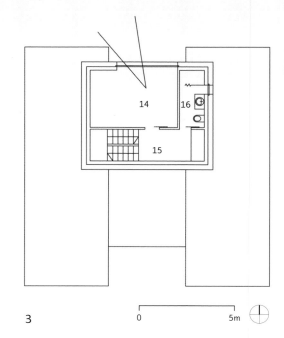

3

0   5m

4

5

6

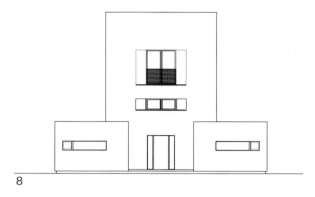

8

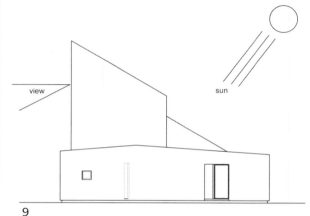

9

7

6 Entrance
7 Interior: set-in glazed patio
8 North elevation
9 West elevation
10 South view
11 Southwest detail
12 'Black box' detail
13 West view

Photography: Tomek Pikula

10

11

12

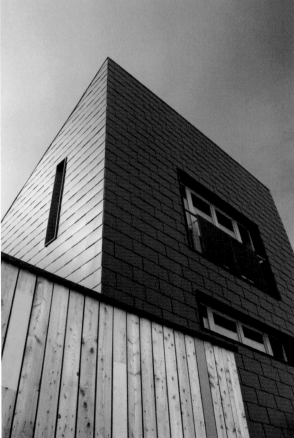

13

COMANO HOUSE
TICINO, SWITZERLAND

DAVIDE MACULLO E MARCO STROZZI ARCHITETTI

Comano is a small village at the foot of a hill 5 kilometres north of Lugano in Ticino. The steeply sloped site inspired the architect to treat the land as a built volume, so that it became part of the architecture of the house.

The construction stands on the lower part of the steep slope, its two vertical volumes organically integrating with the landscape. These volumes were built according to strict regulations regarding building height in order to preserve the view of the historic village on top of the hill. The arrangement of the levels links every room, visually and physically, and enhances the feeling of being continually at ground level. The huge entrance porch, which also functions as covered car park, is carved, cave-like, into the hill leaving the upper volume 'floating' in the green landscape. The void between the main volumes hosts the stairs, which link the shifted levels at different heights and offer the feeling of walking on the natural slope.

The house is composed of three concrete boxes with flat roofs and one glass box for the patio. Each level is shifted by half a storey allowing rational adherence to the land's slope and reducing the excavation required. All indoor spaces are directly linked to their outdoor counterparts, enhancing the perception of being constantly in touch with nature. Exterior spaces of concrete, grass and water are treated as a continuation of the interior via clear geometric lines.

This house was planned to ensure intimacy and privacy, allowing the inhabitants to enjoy the beautiful surrounding landscape without being visible from outside. The design affords shadowed spaces in summer and glazed winter gardens, which absorb radiant heat from the sun in winter to save energy.

Opposite   View from south

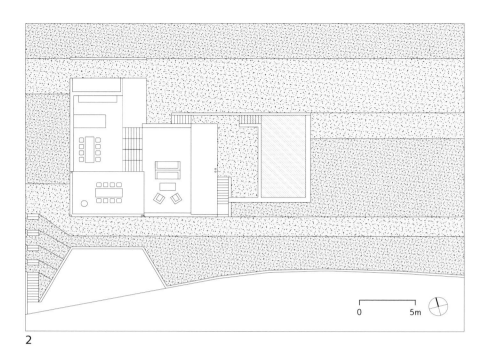

2

4

3

2   Floor plan
3   View from north
4   View from east
5   Void over living room from dining room
6   Dining room and lower landing

Photography: Pino Musi, Enrico Cano

COURT ESSINGTON ESTATE

THE COTSWOLDS, UNITED KINGDOM

DAVID ARCHER ARCHITECTS

Set within the grounds of a 1-hectare estate in the Cotswolds countryside, Court Essington is an extensive Arts & Crafts country manor that has been dramatically remodelled by London-based practice David Archer Architects.

The refurbishment of this house, which dates from 1909, is the second phase of a two-year project following the renovation of the smaller neighbouring guesthouse, The Coach House, completed in 2005. Combined, the two projects offer a contemporary reinterpretation of a 19th-century house and grounds. Both properties command impressive views of the gardens and countryside beyond. Central to the scheme has been the reconfiguration of the conservatory on the south elevation of both houses to frame the revitalised landscape.

The Coach House extension is strikingly modern with a cantilevered frame of solid oak beams simplifying the forms of the existing building. Replacement of the garage door with a picture window on the entrance elevation creates a vista through the house to the new glazed elevation, further accentuating the framed views of the grounds to the rear. Roof decking creates a higher vantage point from which to survey the grounds.

The main house extension is more sympathetic to the style of the original architecture, with a pitched roof and parapet echoing the period features of the house. The timber, glass and stone extension abuts the south elevation, creating a new garden conservatory accessed via the main reception spaces.

Inside the house many of the property's original Edwardian features remain and have been restored to their original condition, invoking the character of the original house. The principal entertaining room, a generous 11 by 7 metres, features a stupendous vault ceiling that has been restored and dramatised by painting the end elevation deep red. The morning room is refurbished with white-painted panelling and the kitchen resembles a 1930s creamery, featuring a large central table for family dining, an Aga and an island unit.

Rooms on the south side of the property are decorated in a light palette of warm whites, reflecting the sunshine from the south-facing conservatory. When moving deeper into the plan the palette intensifies, with decorative gold wallpaper along the corridor, ochre yellow in the pantry, card-room green in the library and polka-dot wallpaper in the master and guest bedrooms.

1   *The new conservatory extension with pitched roof and parapet echoing the period features of the house*
2   *The timber, glass and stone extension*
3   *The principal entertaining room*
4   *The kitchen has been completely modernised in the style of a 1930s creamery*

Photography: Keith Collie

THE DAIRY HOUSE

SOMERSET, UNITED KINGDOM

SKENE CATLING DE LA PEÑA

Situated on a 345-hectare estate in Somerset, United Kingdom, this project involved the conversion of a former dairy into a five-bedroom house with a small pool. The brief was to combine privacy and seclusion with openness to the wider landscape. The space was to be re-planned pragmatically: lean-to sheds removed and an extension added to create a total of four to five bedrooms, three bathrooms and more generous circulation space with rooms of better proportions. The intervention appears as a natural, discreet extension of the existing structure. Sources of inspiration were both literal, as in the stacked timber in the yard opposite, and literary, as in the 18th-century architectural treatise and erotic novella by Jean-Francois de Bastide *La Petite Maison – An Architectural Seduction*.

The extension houses two bathrooms and everything behind the retaining wall can be flooded with water. Layered oak and laminated float glass produce an eerie, filtered light. The dematerialising effects of refraction and reflection create the effect of an aquatic underworld. The way the light moves around the house over the course of the day draws the user through it. In the morning low light floods the east and the glass acts as a prism that projects watery green lozenges over floors and walls. By midday the sun is overhead, streaming through the roof light slot and penetrating the two-way mirror bridge providing views from the ground floor through the building. At night this is reversed, and the flames in the fireplace are visible through the floor of the landing.

The aim was to use as many local materials as possible. Estate timber is planked and dried in the storage barns in the farmyard opposite the site, and the method of drying – where raw planks are separated by spacers to allow air circulation – became the generator of the logic and aesthetic of the extension. The glass was layered in the same manner. The pieces increase in depth towards the base to reinforce a sense of weight and rustication.

Rather than demolishing and rebuilding, the sense of 'retreat' was reinforced through 'camouflage'; the form and massing of the extension echoes and complements the existing structure. The house appears unchanged from the outside, but reveals itself on entering, defying expectations.

1   *Ground floor plan*
2   *First floor plan*
3   *Extension and pool view at night*
4   *View of living room from entrance hall showing slot between old and new structures*
5   *View from access path showing two-way mirror wall*
6   *Master bathroom showing interior view of laminated glass and oak wall*

Photography: © James Morris

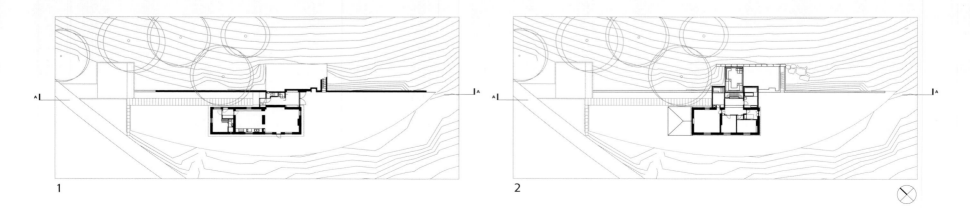

1   2

DRIFT BAY HOUSE

LAKE WAKATIPU, OTAGO, NEW ZEALAND

KERR RITCHIE

This family home was designed as a single fluid form that reclines into the sloping landscape on the edge of Lake Wakatipu. The long black form shifts and expands to suit the sun, the site and the occupants' needs.

The entry is through a hole punched in the middle of the volume, which also creates a courtyard. This allows visitors to enter either the family home to the north or the studio/guest wing to the south. The main house pulls away from the eastern bank to provide courtyards sheltered from the prevailing wind and summer sun. It then expands upwards to form a double-level volume, maximising engagement with the northern sun. The house rises up again to the studio, at the 'tail', before snaking back towards the sun and the north.

The roof and walls of the house are primarily clad in black steel. However, the entry and the areas where the occupants move in and out of the house to the north and south elevations are clad with softer timber boards.

The interior is intended to have the resilience of an institutional building. Robust concrete floors collect the warmth of the sun, and profiled insitu concrete walls and strandboard are softened with a shiny plastic glowing screen wall and plastic light fittings. Space and forms shift up and down to create spaces that move from snug to lofty and back again.

Opposite   The edge of Lake Wakatipu provides both an alpine and subtropical environment

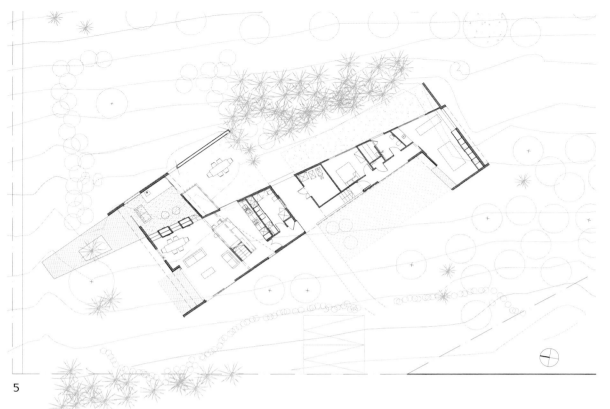

2   *Casual rock walls and paths surround the home and intertwine with a rambling native garden*

3   *The house pulls away from the steep landscape providing a sheltered eastern courtyard that links to the kitchen through a sliding door*

4   *The cedar-clad entry to the studio wing*

5   *Lower level plan*

6   *The family area is divided into two spaces – an open living/dining space and a separate cosy lounge*

7   *The strandboard-clad stairwell is used to delineate the double-height kitchen space from the living areas*

Photography: Paul McCredie

DUBLIN BAY HOUSE

WANAKA, OTAGO, NEW ZEALAND

SALMOND ARCHITECTURE

This family home is inspired by the simple rural stone buildings of Otago and is sited to maximise sun and views to Lake Wanaka. It is a high-performance house that uses passive solar design and a high level of insulation to ensure energy efficiency and year-round comfort.

Existing deciduous trees provide shade in summer and a sunroom provides shelter from prevailing winds. The sunroom also collects heat to distribute to the rest of the house during autumn and spring. The narrow plan suits the long narrow site and ensures good daylighting and cross ventilation to all spaces. The spacious main living area opens up on three sides, connecting the house to the site and allowing the room to expand to the outdoors in summer.

Natural materials have been selected for low maintenance, appearance and durability. Solar panels supply hot water and the house has an independent water supply and waste treatment facility.

While the Dublin Bay House is simple and traditional in form to suit its context and the family's needs, it is also energy efficient, low maintenance, comfortable and designed to perform well throughout its life.

1

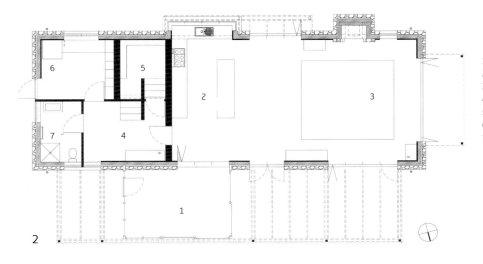

1	Entry
2	Kitchen
3	Living
4	Hall
5	Cellar
6	Laundry
7	Bathroom

2

1   West elevation showing living room doors open,
    main bedroom above

2   Ground floor plan

3   Sunroom from the entry door

4   Living room and sunroom open to garden
    and views

5   Structural bookshelves flank the stairwell

Photography: Nigel Young, Square Circle

3

5

4

EAGLE BAY RESIDENCE

EAGLE BAY, WESTERN AUSTRALIA, AUSTRALIA

CHINDARSI ARCHITECTS

Holidays on the Indonesian island of Bali inspired the owners' brief for their new home on a large clear block overlooking the Indian Ocean at Eagle Bay, a three-hour drive south of Perth.

The house was designed as a family compound, based on a single-level courtyard model. As such, the plan focuses on private courtyard spaces that are sheltered from the area's strong sea breezes. Simultaneously, the house was built up on its site in order to take advantage of ocean views to the north.

The design incorporates generous living spaces and bedrooms for the owners' four children as well as a separate self-contained studio for their grandmother, a gymnasium, a sauna, lap and wading pools and a tennis court. Passive solar design principles were incorporated into the overall design, with generous eaves and blade walls for sun shading.

The local limestone used for the walls as well as the timber flooring and decking are in keeping with the relaxed vernacular of the area. The design influences behind the Eagle Bay residence are many and varied: among them are Frank Lloyd Wright's Robie House and Mies van der Rohe's brick Case Study house along with Eastern influences and a touch of the traditional Australian verandah house.

1 View of alfresco area and northern garden
2 Entry garden at night
3 Blade walls and entry steps towards gate

1

2

3

7

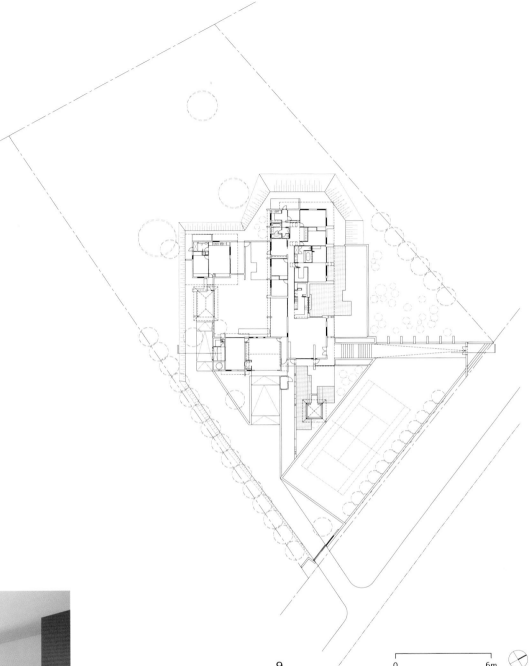

9

0   6m

8

4   *Garden with peppermint tree*

5   *View from pool deck over tennis court*

6   *View within central courtyard*

7   *Lap pool and pavilion towards house*

8   *Kitchen viewed from main living*

9   *Site plan*

Photography: Adrian Lambert - Acorn Photo Agency

EDWARD RIVER RESIDENCE

DENILIQUIN, NEW SOUTH WALES, AUSTRALIA

JACKSON CLEMENTS BURROWS PTY LTD ARCHITECTS

The design of this farmhouse explores an interpretation of historic local farm buildings, which are typically constructed using timber frames and corrugated iron cladding. The two-storey house is sited adjacent to the river and linked to a water tank tower, which identifies its position nestled amongst the indigenous red gums on the river frontage.

The plan is arranged within a regular grid of primary structural columns of laminated cypress. This expression references traditional construction methods and presents an artificial 'forest' of columns that engages with the surrounding eucalypts on the river frontage.

External hardwood timber purlins are visually revealed to the inside face of the corrugated iron cladding to extend the reference to traditional shed construction techniques. The extensive areas of Western red cedar cladding and Western red cedar doors and windows finished in ebony stain accentuate the contrast between concrete, steel and corrugated iron and provide another level of interest and detail.

Internally, the house challenges traditional farmhouse planning. While the practical aspects of the farmhouse program are located on the ground the floor (boot room, laundry, garage and workshop), the primary living areas are located on the first floor to take advantage of views of the river frontage and surrounding paddocks.

The Edward River Residence engages with its context to provide a fitting architectural solution that extends the relevance of traditional timber construction techniques.

1   *The design of the house extends from an interpretation of local rural farm buildings*
2   *Covered entry suspended under header tank*

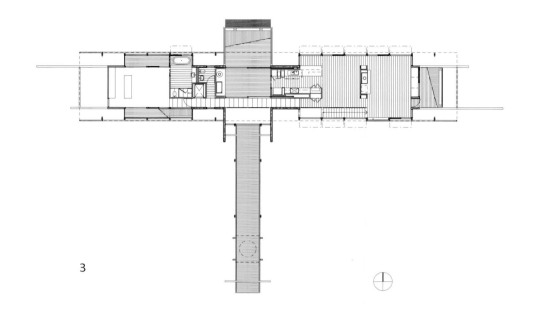

3

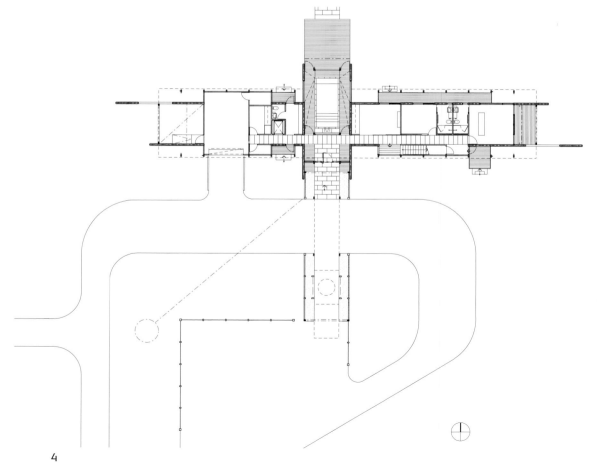

4

5

6

3 First floor plan

4 Ground floor plan

5 Double-height void to entry area assists passive cooling

6 Indoor pool acts as a cooling element in central breezeway

7 Outdoor gauze room

8 Galley kitchen connecting to gauze room

Photography: Jon Clements

FERROUS HOUSE

SPRING PRAIRIE, WISCONSIN, USA

JOHNSEN SCHMALING ARCHITECTS

The Ferrous House sits on the edge of a wooded nature preserve in a rural area west of Milwaukee. Designed on top of an existing dwelling that had fallen into serious disrepair, the building's simple rectangular volume provides 130 square metres of living space and is wrapped on three sides with a suspended curtain of weathering steel panels. The warm colour of ferrous corrosion on the panels echoes the hues of the derelict farm equipment left behind on the area's abandoned pastures. The steel wrapper protects the inside of the house from the scrutiny of suspicious neighbours and the elements; at the back, it extends beyond the building's perimeter, where it shelters the sides of a linear south-facing patio.

Linear storage boxes containing built-in closet systems and living room cabinetry penetrate the steel curtain and cantilever over the edge of the building, adding desperately needed floor space without altering the original footprint of the house.

In a carefully choreographed entry sequence, wide exterior stairs run along the front of the house and lead into a glazed foyer, an extension of the main circulation core that transforms into a small observatory above the roof. The slightly tilted roof plane is supported by a filigree of exposed metal and wood trusses, adding height to the living spaces and allowing northern light to wash the inside of the house through a translucent, Nanogel-filled glass band. At night, the window band radiates its warm light into the distance, subtly evoking the iconic clerestory glow of the dairy barns that once dotted the region.

The Ferrous House offers a resource-conscious solution to the challenges of an aging stock of rural housing. In contrast to a radical tabula rasa approach, the project demonstrates how the bones of an obsolete building can be utilised and transformed into the framework for a contemporary countryside dwelling.

1

2

3

4

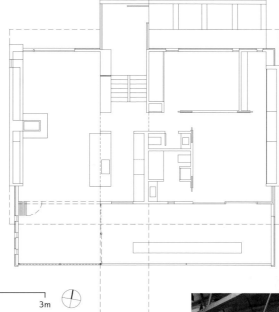

5   *View of living hall with exposed roof trusses*
6   *Floor plan*
7   *View of kitchen*
8   *In the observatory*

Photography: Doug Edmunds

0   3m

6

7

8

FISHERS ISLAND HOUSE

FISHERS ISLAND, NEW YORK, USA

CENTERBROOK ARCHITECTS AND PLANNERS

This is a summer house for a client with many friends. The brief required a Victorian cottage full of good humour, yet relaxed enough to offer a sense of 'shabby gentility'. The site, however, is not so relaxed. High on Fishers Island, New York, it is windswept with low scrub oak all around. Therefore, the house needed to offer a sense of shelter. Inside, the owner wanted many rooms to give guests privacy on crowded weekends, despite the limited budget. Thus, rooms had to be small and varied.

Approached from the west, the house appears as a tribe of connected buildings – a brood of structures surrounding a 'mother house' sharing a family resemblance in cedar shingle siding, dark gable roofs and random 'crazy quilt' stickwork. A porte-cochère (created by the extending the storage shed's roof over the driveway) leads into a small gravel court where the main house looks at a 'drunken' fence to the south. The house's gable faces have gabled windows, the lone consistency in a random placement. A wide cornice band under the eaves is punctuated by tall regular polychrome brackets.

The meandering exterior structures only hint at the colliding spaces inside. Here, within taut exterior walls, formally shaped rooms are placed in balanced chaos like shaken blocks within a toy box. The cylindrical, elliptical, cubical and rectangular volumes are comfortable – functional, familiar and easy to live with – but their union is full of tension, offering extraordinary spatial changes and new vistas at each doorway.

1   East façade
2   Elliptical living room has stickwork cornice and mantle
3   North façade overlooks Fishers Island Sound
4   First floor plan

Photography: Timothy Hursley

1

3

2

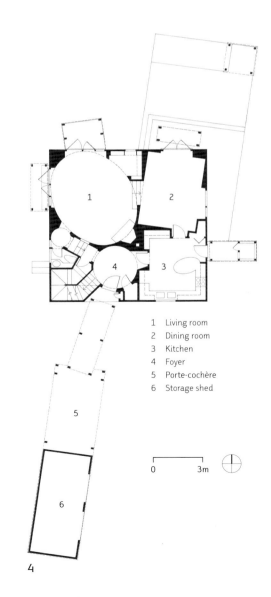

1 Living room
2 Dining room
3 Kitchen
4 Foyer
5 Porte-cochère
6 Storage shed

0 _____ 3m

5

6

4

FLOYD HOUSE

CONNECTICUT RIVER, CONNECTICUT, USA

CENTERBROOK ARCHITECTS AND PLANNERS

Floyd House is a new 180-square-metre home on a half-hectare waterfront site in a Connecticut River village. It looks out over an anchorage with a view of tidal marshes and distant hills.

The house is a paean to the 19th-century packet boat vernacular that arose prior to the great steamboat era – a tradition researched by the architect. The era is characterised by flat-bottomed shanty boats, stick-built packet boats and informal wharf boats, which rode the rise and fall of the water tied to docks for convenient loading. Many of the packet boats had flat hulls supporting two storeys of porch-like wooden decks. The decks wrapped enclosed superstructures housing symmetrically arranged cargo spaces, staterooms, dining rooms, staircases and lounges, many with elaborate wood details.

Evoking this long-lost river vernacular, the house is entered between a pair of wharf-like sheds to which it is conceptually moored. It sits above the flood plain on a wrap-around deck, the ground gathered beneath it like a rising tide. In the wharf boat tradition the house is a slope-roofed box, but in the packet boat tradition the box is wrapped in two-storey decks. A monitor and chimney sit atop the roof, not unlike the interlocking crew quarters and wheelhouses that were typical of packet boats. The design intention was to mix these 19th-century vernaculars to create a house subliminally suited to its riverfront setting.

Modest bedrooms are placed on the first level, and public rooms are on the second where they have bigger volumes, enjoy views and capture breezes. Interior finishes employ marine paint, plantation mahogany brightwork and brass fittings in ways that, like the house's exterior, take their cue from this now-lost American tradition.

1   *The house sits above the flood plain on a wrap-around deck*
2   *The rooftop monitor captures and reflects daylight within the living areas on the second floor*
3   *The living room, shown here, and other public rooms are on the second floor where they enjoy views and capture breezes*
4   *Porches flanking the north and south sides of the house provide natural heating and cooling to the main living areas*
5   *Second floor plan*

Photography: Jeff Goldberg / Esto

1

3

2

4

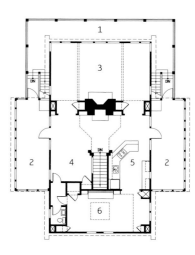

5

1 Deck
2 Porch
3 Living room
4 Dining room
5 Kitchen
6 Family room
7 Garage
8 Art studio

0   5m

FOOTHILLS HOUSE

POKENO, NORTH WAIKATO, NEW ZEALAND

SGA LTD (STRACHAN GROUP ARCHITECTS)

Nestled on the lower southern slopes of the Bombay Hills and overlooking the Whangamarino Wetlands, the Foothills House epitomises New Zealand living for a young family with historic roots in this small rural community. With panoramic views of the Waikato countryside to the south and east and a high level of exposure to the often-harsh southwesterly winds, the site provided an interesting and often conflicting functional challenge to occupation.

The low-slung roof form follows the topography of the land, presenting a low profile that deflects and protects against the strong winds that accelerate across the valley floor. This simple roof extends over an elongated plan that stretches parallel to the land contour, offering sheltered courtyards and verandahs to the north and extending a strong axis to the northeast, which in turn provides a prospect towards a lush native bush reserve.

The building comprises two elongated shed-like pavilions defining the living areas from the private areas and an internal garden courtyard linking the two. Arrival and entry is guided by stone-clad walls through a foyer located towards the southern end of the lower pavilion. The foyer separates a home office and garage and storage areas on the left from the main living spaces on the right. An enclave living room opens onto an open-plan kitchen, dining and sitting area with direct connections to the pool, verandah and courtyard. Ribbon windows along the entire southeastern wall allow panoramic landscape views to the Coromandel Ranges. Directly ahead from the main entry foyer, the stone wall gives way to an internal courtyard – a linking space with broad steps to the upper pavilion housing the bedrooms, service areas and gymnasium.

The site demanded the use of a palette of durable materials – coated steel, zinc, stone and concrete masonry. Cedar weatherboards are used in their raw state to blend with the natural landscape. Eco-friendly features include passive solar heating, natural ventilation and cooling, rainwater harvesting for general and potable uses and on-site wastewater treatment.

1

4

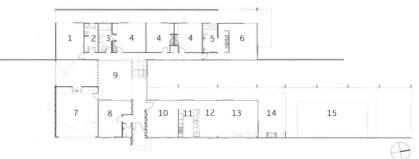

1	Gym	6	Master bedroom	11	Kitchen
2	Laundry	7	Garage	12	Dining
3	Bathroom	8	Study	13	Family
4	Bedroom	9	Internal courtyard	14	Covered terrace
5	Ensuite	10	Living	15	Pool

5

6

3   Family room and courtyard

4   Floor plan

5   Internal courtyard

6   Master bedroom and northern façade colonnade

Photography: Patrick Reynolds and Victor Chia

FORMENTERA ISLAND HOME AND OFFICE

ES PUJOL DE S'ERA, FORMENTERA, SPAIN

MARIÀ CASTELLÓ

Es Pujol de s'Era is a typical rural area on the island of Formentera. It comprises some 33,000 square metres of wheat and barley fields and scrubland of savin, rosemary and juniper.

This home and office, a strictly geometrical 12- by 12-metre structure, nestles between the existing vegetation and the remnant of a traditionally crafted drystone wall. The wall establishes the building's alignment on the site. Similarly, an old 'cistern chapel' determines the longitudinal axis. The architecture echoes the traditional Formentera vernacular, while avoiding mimicry. The design's north–south orientation creates a duality and separates public activity from private life. The office is located in the northernmost part, which is also the most exposed side. Natural northern light floods the space throughout the day, avoiding any sense of confinement.

The house was planned as a refuge; it opens up fully to the south in search of the sun, pursuing maximum interaction between interior and exterior. From indoors, the small wood is perceived as a natural garden providing considerable seclusion and privacy.

A nucleus of service areas is set between the studio and the house, physically separating the owner's work life and private life yet providing shared elements of 'infrastructure': the library, filing system, bathroom, kitchen, beds, cupboards, machinery and two sliding partitions that enable the two main zones to be separated.

The elevation is slightly staggered along the perimeter, giving the impression that the building is hovering above the ground. The envelope is made of coated thermo-clay blocks and reinforced concrete; an extruded section is the only part of the building that involved 'wet' construction. The remaining interior and exterior walls were dry built using glass and iroko wood. The side openings present as incisions slicing the façade open from top to bottom, fragmenting the east and west elevations and reducing their bulk.

1   Floor plan
2   The house is oriented south in a small wood
3   Office interior
4   The nucleus contains the beds and other elements
5   Interior: the majority of the furniture was custom designed for this project

Photography: Marià Castelló (1,3,4,5); Lourdes Grivé (2)

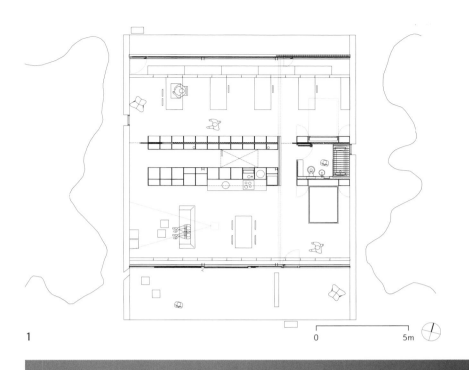

1

3

4

2

5

FOXGROUND RESIDENCE

FOXGROUND, NEW SOUTH WALES, AUSTRALIA

STUDIOINTERNATIONALE

This contemporary country residence was designed for a design-savvy retired couple on their 24-hectare rural property in Foxground, approximately 104 kilometres south of Sydney.

Conceived as part of studiointernationale's 'platform1234' modular building system, the design extends the possibilities of a modular solution, creating a generously proportioned and casually sophisticated country retreat.

A meandering gravel driveway runs off a narrow country lane, and works its way through the changing terrain of natural bushland to cleared paddocks and the house near the southern boundary.

The residence is configured as a series of pavilions with an L-shaped plan, oriented to maximise solar access and panoramic mountain views to the north and west. Entry is gained via a raised semi-enclosed deck, which separates the living pavilion (with an east-west axis) from the bedroom pavilions (with a north-south axis). A simple zinc-clad garage accommodates two cars and the plant room and is separated from the living pavilion at ground level by a water garden.

The living pavilion contains an entry/gallery space, a study, an open-plan kitchen and a dining and living area with a zinc-clad pod concealing the laundry/guest bathroom and walk-in pantry. A sculptural, telescopic circular fireplace hangs between the living and dining areas punctuating the otherwise uninterrupted view through the open space to the vast landscape beyond.

Separate sleeping pavilions – one housing the main bedroom and the other housing two guest bedrooms – are connected via a semi-enclosed deck with direct access to the 25-metre raised stone lap pool. The main bedroom pavilion has a leather-clad blade wall, separating the 'milky' glass-clad ensuite and walk-in robe from the bedroom area. The guest bedroom pavilion has two bedrooms, each with ensuite and generous wardrobes.

The pavilions are raised off the ground and have an expressed steel structure in-filled with pre-weathered zinc cladding on the south and east façades, and glazed panels to the north and west. The north and west façades have floor-to-ceiling operable glazing with sun protection through retractable, motorised external aluminium louvres. A low-profile cantilevered roof extends over the building, sheltering it from the elements and providing undercover walkways around the pavilions.

The buildings are naturally ventilated with good solar access and sun protection and have a sustainable water supply through underground water tanks and onsite wastewater management.

1

1 Lap pool with wet edge looking towards the
   bedroom pavilion
2 Deck overlooking lap pool
3 Dusk shot of pool looking towards living pavilions

2

3

4 *Entry deck looking towards the garage*
5 *Breezeway through sleeping pavilion*
6 *Floor plan*
7 *Lounge with suspended telescopic fireplace*
8 *Open-plan dining and kitchen area*
9 *Guest bedroom opening to northern deck*

Photography: © Martin van der Wal

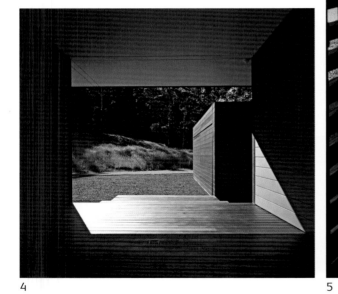

4

5

6

1 Deck
2 Guest bedroom
3 Bathroom
4 Main bedroom
5 Walk-in robe
6 Entry stairs
7 Garage
8 Water garden
9 Study
10 Entry gallery
11 Reading area
12 Laundry/guest bathroom
13 Pantry
14 Kitchen
15 Dining
16 Fireplace
17 Lounge
18 Lap pool

9

7

8

GIDGEGANNUP RESIDENCE

GIDGEGANNUP, WESTERN AUSTRALIA, AUSTRALIA

IREDALE PEDERSEN HOOK ARCHITECTS

Gidgegannup is a small semi-rural setting approximately 40 minutes' drive northeast of Perth. This project began as a delicate line in the landscape occupying the space between the ground and the sky. This delicate line transforms into a sequence of platforms for observing the landscape. The experience of inhabitation is enriched by the potential to manipulate ways of observing place and landscape.

The house stretches between a large body of native trees on the edge of the property and a mature tree that touches the cantilevering balcony of the main bedroom.

While moving through the house one experiences the natural context in a variety of ways. At times these are specifically framed views and at other times they are abstracted views of the landscape. These views sometimes create a sense of connection to the ground and at other times a distinct desire to hover above the ground. The connection to the ground is simultaneously delicate and brutal, the hovering house and balcony acts as a counterpoise to the semi-embedded pool and spa.

The design makes full and sometimes dramatic use of the existing site contours. The pool is placed 1200 millimetres above the external ground level to conform to regulations. This is the only section of manipulated land in the design; the rest attempts to minimise the home's impact on and modification of the natural contours.

The form of the building and selection of materials responds to a distinct farming aesthetic. Initially the owners desired a house that looked more like a slick city dwelling, but the architect suggested an alternative approach that involved a sophisticated manipulation of the local vernacular. This evolved into the final design – an appropriate response to the place.

The house has numerous sustainable features. Rainwater is collected for all domestic needs and the timbers used in construction came from managed plantations. External window treatments were designed to minimise heat gain in summer and maximise heat gain in winder. The floor is heavily insulated to reduce the impact of the external temperature.

In 2008, World Architecture News (WAN) named the Gidgegannup Residence as one of its Top 30 Houses of the Year.

1   Seen from the distance, the house hovers as a delicate line in the landscape
2   The house hovers above the ground making dramatic use of the existing contours
3   Materials and form were developed from the surrounding farming aesthetic and technology

1

3

2

4

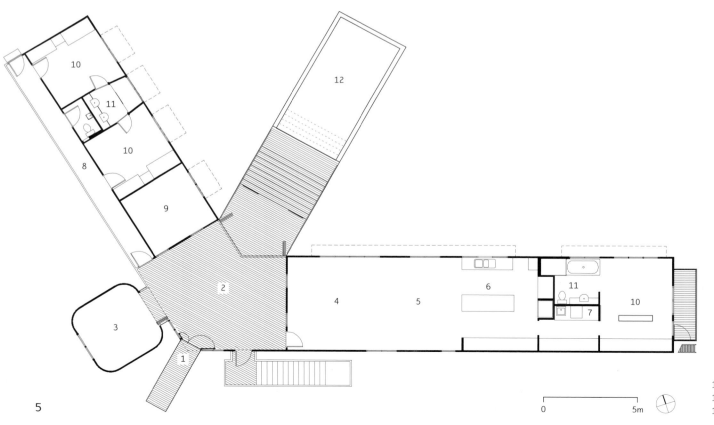

5

4   Arrival is from above, where the
    house cranks to embrace the
    landscape

5   Floor plan

6   The children's rooms are accessed
    via a polycarbonate-clad passage
    that abstracts the native trees

7   The living space opens to the foyer
    and music room allowing sound to
    filter through the house

8   The foyer is a flexible space that
    can be opened to the landscape
    and living spaces

Photography: Patrick Bingham-Hall

1   Entry
2   Family room
3   Music room
4   Lounge
5   Dining
6   Kitchen
7   Laundry
8   Corridor
9   TV room
10 Bedroom
11 Bathroom
12 Pool

0   5m

1   Floor plan
2   Heavy masonry wall supports light timber structure
3   Northern façade with stone plinth
4   Front verandah showing view of surrounding property
5   Main living area with stone fireplace as anchor to the space

Photography: Shannon McGrath

GREAT WALL OF WARBURTON

WARBURTON, VICTORIA, AUSTRALIA

BKK ARCHITECTS

On an elevated site set amongst native bushland with rolling views to the north, this house withholds the view upon approach, presenting instead a mute, split-faced concrete block wall embedded in the site. The wall and the existing topography form a protected courtyard space that explores BKK's continuing interest in the relationship between building and landscape through a type of 'embedded occupation'.

A compressed entry opens out to reveal a panoramic view of the mountains to the north. Rooms are anchored along the subtly shifting wall, so that spaces unfold when moving through the house. Each interior space becomes a framing device and there is a subtly different outlook from each room. The main living spaces open out onto the pool, spa and pond with views of the mountains beyond.

A double-sided fireplace acts as a divider between the living and dining areas. The entry, kitchen and dining areas are tiled with Castlemaine slate. External and internal timber walls are radial-sawn silvertop ash battens and shiplapped boards, while the internal timber veneer is Sassafras red heart. The rich, warm finishes continue beyond the glass lines and this blurring of boundaries contributes to the sense of immersion within the landscape.

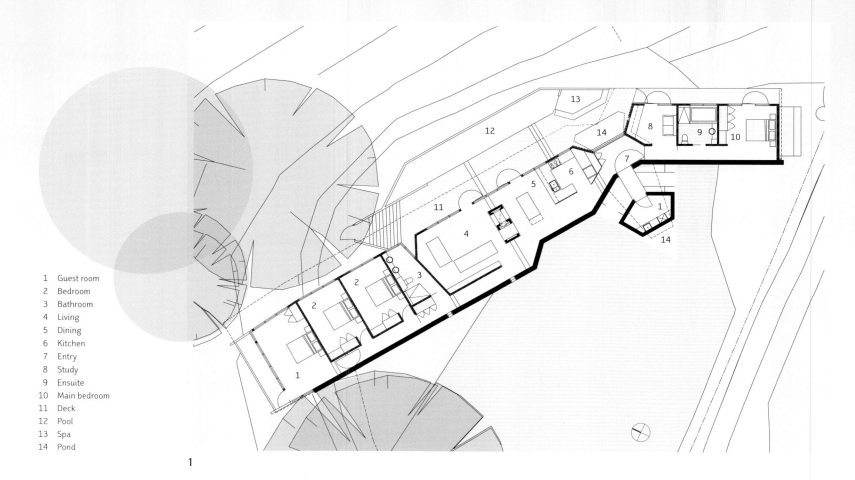

1   Guest room
2   Bedroom
3   Bathroom
4   Living
5   Dining
6   Kitchen
7   Entry
8   Study
9   Ensuite
10 Main bedroom
11 Deck
12 Pool
13 Spa
14 Pond

1

GUESTHOUSE/GALLERY IN KIYOSATO

KIYOSATO, YAMANASHI PREFECTURE, JAPAN

SATOSHI OKADA ARCHITECTS

This project is a guesthouse with an art gallery for private art collections. The brief was for 'a house of art' in a forest. The owner, a banker who has lived abroad for many years, had long dreamed of building a facility to share his collections of art and ancient Buddhist sculptures with friends.

The site is located on the southeast foothill of Mount Yatsugatake, 1300 metres above sea level, where dense coniferous woods sprawl across the land. The site's terrain slopes 4 metres down from west to east. A stream runs along the east boundary, adjacent to a pristine, primeval forest that has been strictly protected. The 207-square-metre volume lies loosely among the trees giving it a fragmented appearance.

The design began with four curved lines, which the architect arbitrarily drew in his sketchbook during a flight to New York. When he drew the four lines, he imagined a major space defined by curved surfaces. Each line turns to form a ship-shaped figure, or 'secondary space', which contains one or more functions. These secondary spaces embrace the kitchen, cocktail area, restroom, stairs, chimney, storage, closet and gallery.

The primary space is conceived as a passage. Because the ship-shaped elements are intricately inclined, the passage becomes a switchback space in which a series of fragmented spatial scenes slide from one view to another, simultaneously previewing and reviewing. Every turning point in the passage is opened visually with a transparent glass wall, allowing enjoyment of the surrounding forest outside.

1   Exterior view from the northeast
2   Façade
3   Exterior view from the northwest

4

5

4   *View of entrance hall on the right, ramp to library on the left*

5   *View from living to dining*

6   *View from dining to living*

7   *Ground floor plan*

8   *Skylit living area*

9   *View to living from entrance hall*

Photography: Satoshi Okada Architects (1,2,4,8);
Koichi Torimura - Nacasa & Partners (3,5,6,9)

8

6

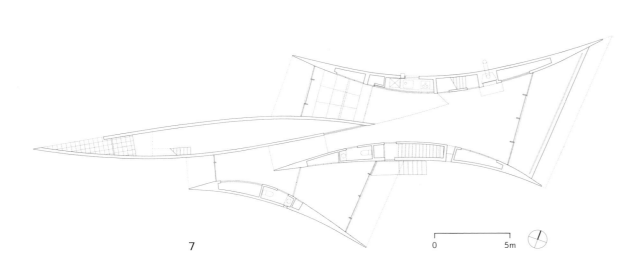

7

0   5m

9

Photography: Christoph Kraneburg

HAUS WOHLFAHRT-LAYMANN

TAUNUS HILLS, GERMANY

MEIXNER SCHLÜTER WENDT ARCHITEKTEN

This house is situated in the Taunus hills area outside Frankfurt am Main.

After a detailed inspection of the site's original 1930s house, the architect decided to use this picturesque and traditional country cottage as a starting point for further planning. A new shell was built around this house and a new interior and intermediate space created to be used as new room. The position of the shell and its distance from the 'inner' house at different points is dictated by the functional requirements of the ground floor plan. In this way, inner, outer, intermediate and 'un-rooms' in various and sometimes curious forms are generated. Complex and seemingly simple rooms alternate with each other. Paradoxes occur – inside and outside – and perceptions of reality become distorted. A simple and traditional country cottage is dissolved, transformed and simultaneously fortified – in the manner of a metamorphosis.

The solid shell provides an optimum upgrading of the building's physics from the inadequately thin original wooden walls. The inner house becomes a wooden insert, or furnishing, within a shell.

The inner house is broken open where light or space are required for its interior – these 'light connections' and 'space connections' are then projected outwards and transferred onto the shell as perforations. The roof of the original structure is completely open and the rooms in the roof are extended upward with vertical spacing connections.

The dark brown earth covering the garden is symbolically continued inside the house via the dark brown flooring of the terrace and the parquet floor. The grey-green colouring of the outer shell integrates well into the colours of the surrounding woodlands.

1

2

4

3

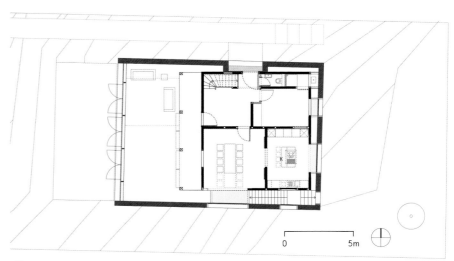

5

HDX WORKSHOP

VALLE DE BRAVO, MEXICO

BGP ARQUITECTURA

This project involved a significant addition to a house designed in 1987 by bgp arquitectura for the same owner. The 140-square-metre addition consists of a guest's quarters and a studio for the owner. Both spaces were conceived as independent volumes with a large terrace that articulates the old house and the new program.

The guest's quarters and the terrace were built in the initial construction phase. The skin of the guest room is a red, channelled plate that creates shadows on the box's surface while contrasting with the dense surrounding vegetation.

Two of the most important issues affecting the design were the owner's reduced budget as well as the need to have minimal construction time. Despite the difference in age between the two buildings, the new project creates an interesting and contrasting dialogue that harmonises with the site and the existing construction.

1

2

4

3

5

6

6   *View from the interior to the landscape exterior*
7   *Longitudinal section*
8   *Main floor plan*
9   *View from the interior to the landscaped exterior*
10 *Detail of the window*

Photography: Rafael Gamo

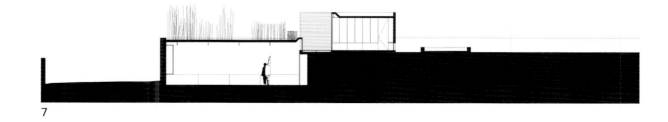

7

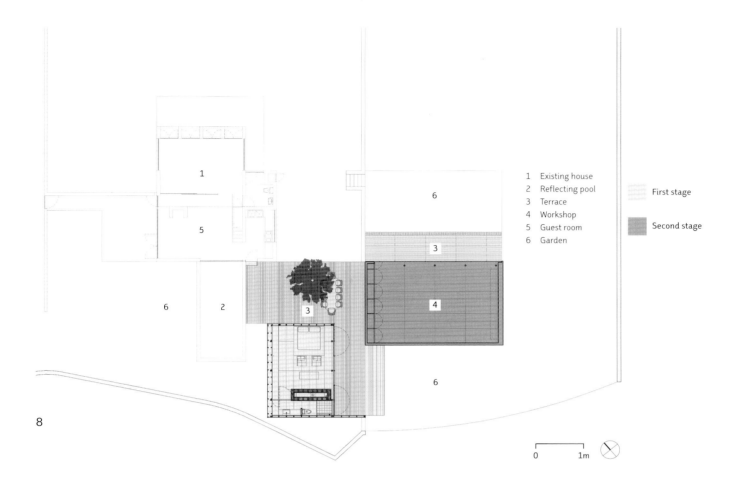

1   Existing house
2   Reflecting pool
3   Terrace
4   Workshop
5   Guest room
6   Garden

First stage

Second stage

0   1m

8

9

10

HOF RESIDENCE

SKAKAFJÖRDUR FJORD, ICELAND

STUDIO GRANDA

Hof is a country residence in the Skakafjördur fjord, less than 100 kilometres from the Arctic Circle. The spectacle of the location, its remoteness and special program fuelled a unique rapport between the client, contractor and architect resulting in a building that reflects every aspect of that collaboration.

The existing assemblage of buildings on the estate includes a house, church, barn and cowshed clustered on a riverbank. Further inland are recently constructed horse stables. The wide fjord has a mountainous rim punctuated with long valleys embracing the cliff islands of Drangey, Málmey and the striking headland of Thordahofdi. The new residence is slightly removed from the old cluster on raised ground, with each room and space designed to capture this magnificent panorama.

The house rises from the tufted site as a series of sheer cedar and concrete walls that will weather according to the vagaries of the elements. The displaced grass of the field is reinstated on the roof and the surrounding meadow is cut and folded in earthworks of turf and stone that open ways to the entrance and terraces. Hexagonal basalt pillars were excavated from the site during the preparations for the foundations and the external surfaces are paved in this material. The same stone is used throughout the living and circulation areas.

Most internal walls are raw or painted concrete and the ceilings, doors and other carpentry are predominately oiled sawn oak with steel details; a rustic palette offset by smooth painted planes. In a gesture of refinement and escapism the kitchen and bathrooms enjoy marble surfaces suggestive of more habitable latitudes whereas the larder's glazed white tiles and basalt shelves evoke the need to store food for harsh winters.

The house is highly insulated and thermally stable due to the massive concrete walls, stone floors and balanced fenestration. Geothermal water is used for the floor heating and radiators as well as for all domestic use. Electricity consumption is minimised by design and the small amount that is required is sourced from hydroelectric and geothermal sources.

Although dramatic views fill the interior, the ambience is augmented by a secondary system of clerestory lights and other roof penetrations that orchestrate daylight throughout the house. The exception is the dogleg route between the living and bedroom wings where lighting is reduced to a few pinpricks.

1   View from southeast
2   View from southwest

3

0   5m

4

Photography: Sigurgeir Sigurjónsson

A HOME IN VALLE D'AOSTA

VALLE D'AOSTA, ITALY

SILVESTRI ARCHITETTURA

With a striking view over one of the most beautiful valleys of Valle d'Ayas in Valle d'Aosta, Italy, this old stone house was restored with the traditional character of local buildings in mind. It is a warm mountain home that interprets the genius loci and the quietness of the surroundings. To this end, the architect decided to keep as much of the ancient building as possible, working very carefully in order not to lose any of its personality. Original features include some exterior stone walls, almost 60 centimetres thick, a marvellous ground floor with a stone vault, and a part of the original roof, with wooden beams and the typical stone covering. To recreate the original atmosphere, the architect used local materials for structures (stone and wood) and the same local stone that has been used for centuries for the roof. All the materials were used raw, with no plaster or paint on the exteriors, apart from any protective painting.

The interiors have the same atmosphere as the exterior and the materials are revealed as much as possible. On the ground floor an old stable has been converted into a kitchen and the beautiful original stone vault has been restored and left visible. The large living room on the upper level has an intriguing proportion and the timber roof structure plays an important role. The windows in the living space open onto the mountains and offer an extraordinary landscape view that becomes part of the interior space. The result is a building perfectly integrated with the local tradition, a house built in continuity with the old village around it and a home that offers an unforgettably relaxing atmosphere in front of the stunning Alps of Valle d'Aosta.

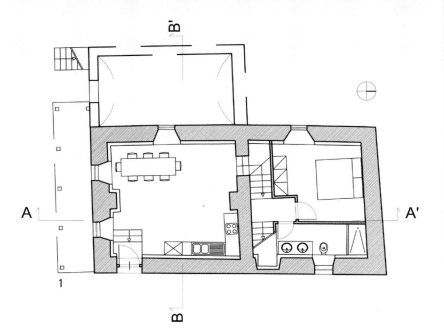

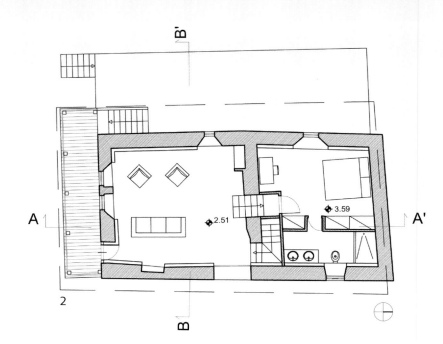

1 Ground floor plan
2 First floor plan
3 The original asymmetrical proportions have been maintained
4 The living room windows open onto the landscape
5 Direct access to the wooden balcony projected towards the front mountain
6 The beautiful vault of the old barn was transformed into the kitchen

Photography: Roberto Silvestri

5

4

6

HOUSE F

KRONBERG, TAUNUS, GERMANY

MEIXNER SCHLÜTER WENDT ARCHITEKTEN

The architect's goal when planning this house was to unite the living rooms with the topography of the idyllic orchard lawn setting. Local authorities stipulated that the roof form must be pitched and, taking cues from the variety of interpretations of this caveat in the surrounding area, the architects developed an original solution that merged the traditional pitched roof typology with the aerodynamic form of a stealth fighter plane.

The new building is subdivided into three zones. The ground floor is completely submerged in the earth, forming a cellar. The garden floor, containing the kitchen and living spaces is embedded in the orchard lawn and opens out to the landscape. Seemingly levitating above the glassed volume of the garden floor, the top floor completes the contours of the pitched-roof house and contains three bedrooms, two bathrooms and a study. Its black sheet-metal cladding blurs the distinction between roof and aircraft. The thin edge of the top floor's wedge form incorporates an automated sunshade system with sections that fold up and down depending on the sun's angle, further referencing the dynamics of a hovering plane.

The floor-to-ceiling glass of the garden floor connects the interior with the orchard lawn in an unbroken flow. Continuing this flow, the orchard lawn features architectural landscaping including a pool and terrace.

2

2   East profile
3   Garden floor plan
4   South elevation
5   Roof closed
6   Roof partially opened
7   Kitchen/living room
8   View from kitchen

Photography: Christoph Kraneburg

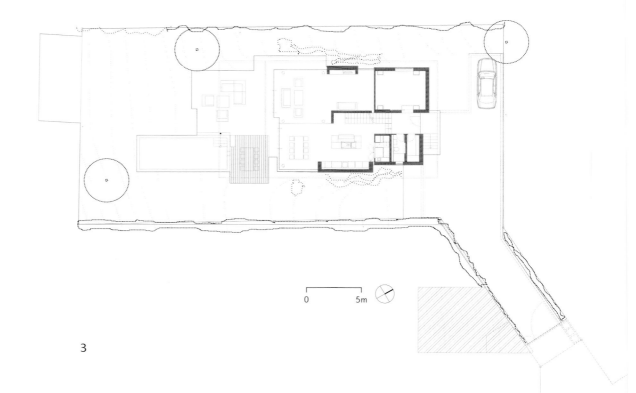

0   5m

3

4

5

6

7

8

HOUSE OCHO

CARMEL VALLEY, CALIFORNIA, USA

FELDMAN ARCHITECTURE

House Ocho sits atop a narrow ridge with old oak groves on either end, a site with steep meadows and commanding views in all directions. The owners originally envisioned a meandering Spanish-style house, but such a scheme meant either tearing out a large number of the site's beautiful oaks or placing the house in the middle of the ridge where it would dominate the site. Above all, the clients had fallen in love with the land and wanted a house that would enhance, not detract from, its natural beauty. At the same time, they wanted a warm, light-filled house with ample space to accommodate many guests at once.

The architect's solution was to position the house in the hillside below a cluster of stunning trees and divide the program into a series of grass-covered pavilions. Sinking the house into the hillside diminished its visual impact and left the oak grove largely untouched. Pulling apart the building elements not only broke up the house's overall massing, but enabled light to penetrate three sides of each element. Additionally, the spaces between the elements became usable outdoor rooms.

A striking feature, and one of the house's many green design elements, is the 'living roof' consisting of native grasses and wildflowers. Photovoltaic skylights are integrated as a primary design element that produces beautiful diffuse light and allows the house, though it is sunk into a hillside, to remain bright and cheery. The home's passive solar heating strategy comprises southeast glass windows and abundant thermal mass from concrete floors and exposed retaining walls. Low-E glass provides maximum insulation without significantly restricting the important solar heat transmission. Another sustainable feature is insulation made from post-industrial cotton fibres and recycled denim. Sandblasted form boards created concrete retaining walls with a soft, silvery, wood-like texture.

1   House Ocho blends seamlessly with its environment
2   The natural landscape is an important element that has been integrated into all aspects of the design
3   The exterior terrace connects the guest rooms to the main house

4

6

7

1   Arrival
2   Entry terrace
3   Entry
4   Family room
5   Powder room
6   Kitchen
7   Dining room
8   Living room
9   Spa
10 Master bedroom
11 Master bathroom
12 Office
13 Loft/access to roof deck
14 Guest bedroom
15 Guest bathroom
16 Mechanical

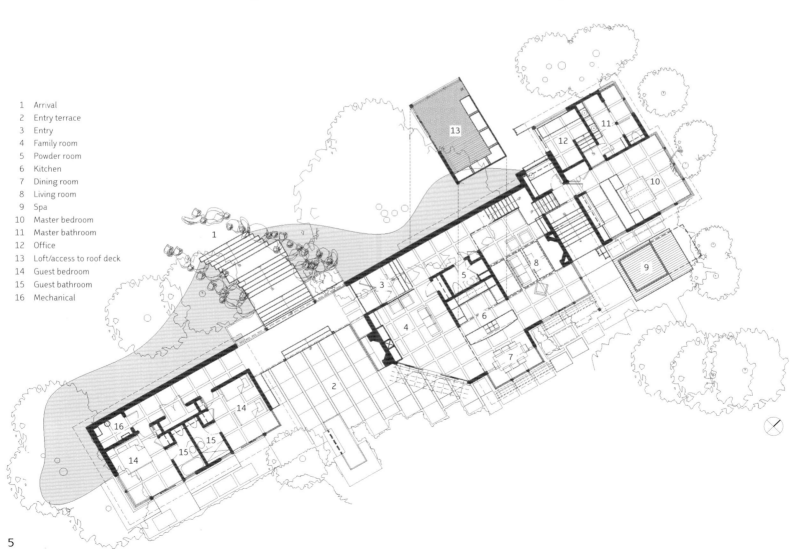

5

4   Natural light streams onto concrete floors as the ceiling
     fans help control the airflow

5   Floor plan

6   An adaptable loft space can be seen nestled above the
     kitchen

7   High ceilings contribute to the feeling of abundant space

8   The large pivot door provides light for the concrete
     thermal mass, contributing to the passive solar strategy

9   The guest bedroom offers visitors the luxury of privacy
     along with landscape views

Photography: Paul Dyer Photography, paul@dyerphoto.com

HOUSE ON EASTERN LONG ISLAND

LONG ISLAND, NEW YORK, USA

ALFREDO DE VIDO

The natural materials used in this house on eastern Long Island, including wood shingles, fences and gates, weather well in the ocean climate and form part of the local vernacular architecture.

The design shows the influence of the architecture of Japan where the architect has lived and worked. In Japan, with its similar oceanic climate, builders have used and revered wood for centuries. The house's sweeping rooflines, detailing, muted palette and the use of wood both externally and internally all reflect the Japanese aesthetic.

Spaces inside the house are open to one another, making them adaptable to the amount of occupants and visitors and able to accommodate a variety of functions.

A detailed dark-wood cornice tracking around the living spaces contrasts with white walls and a dark-wood floor inset with bluestones, echoing the stepping-stones outside.

During construction a storm felled a much-loved tree nearby, so the architect had it sawn into planks that were dried and incorporated into the house design as mantles, ledges and tables.

The flat site is broken up into several distinct areas. They are fenced and unified by bluestone paving and lush, natural vegetation. These areas include an entrance court with ornamental gate and a lily pond, which are both in front of the house, and a sitting area and a secluded swimming pool behind the house.

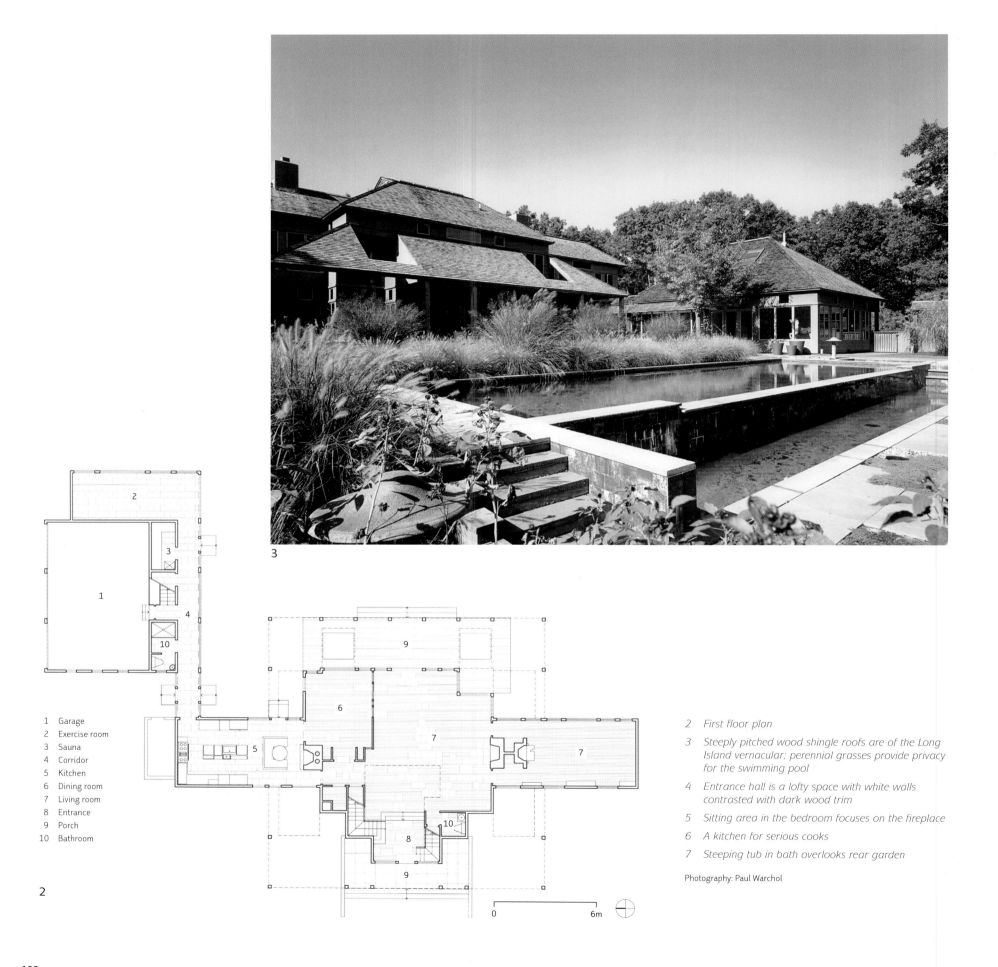

3

1 Garage
2 Exercise room
3 Sauna
4 Corridor
5 Kitchen
6 Dining room
7 Living room
8 Entrance
9 Porch
10 Bathroom

2

2   First floor plan

3   Steeply pitched wood shingle roofs are of the Long
    Island vernacular; perennial grasses provide privacy
    for the swimming pool

4   Entrance hall is a lofty space with white walls
    contrasted with dark wood trim

5   Sitting area in the bedroom focuses on the fireplace

6   A kitchen for serious cooks

7   Steeping tub in bath overlooks rear garden

Photography: Paul Warchol

0   6m

4

5

6

7

HUNTER HOUSE

CAVAN, ONTARIO, CANADA

SCOTT MORRIS ARCHITECTS

The Hunter House is a contemporary, post-and-beam house in a rural setting of 40 hectares. It features many sustainable elements, including passive-solar, off-grid power and straw-bale construction. It is proof that environmentally friendly houses do not need to be traditional in design. The owners of the Hunter House wanted a design that was very modern and progressive – a home that uses the latest technology to transform natural elements into power and that incorporates some very basic, commonsense planning and material choices in order to make the most out of energy.

The passive-solar design incorporates a south-facing, thermally glazed, top-vented gallery, shaded to reduce solar heat gain in summer. The structural frame was constructed of engineered parallel-strand timbers with long-span roof trusses. Exterior walls are composed of affordable and environmentally responsible straw bales. Further eco-friendly features include solar-reflective, long-life, recyclable galvalume roofing panels; roof-mounted photovoltaic and solar water heating systems; natural ventilation and day lighting; an electricity-producing wind turbine and a high-efficiency wood stove.

Superficially, it is impossible to tell that this is a completely self-sufficient house that does not rely on the power grid. Demonstrating that there need not be a choice between going back to nature and the benefit of modern conveniences, the Hunter House enjoys the best of both worlds.

1

3

1   View from south
2   View from southeast
3   View from east

2

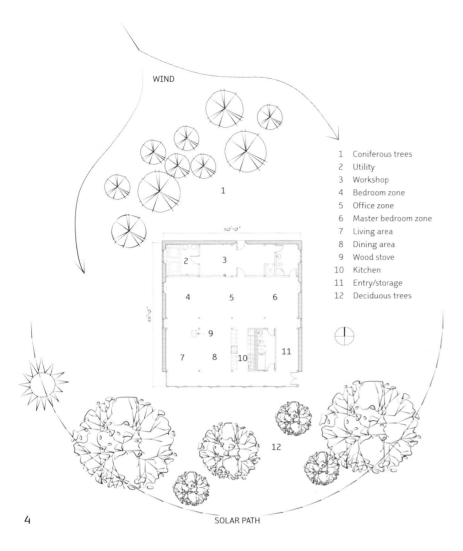

WIND

SOLAR PATH

1 Coniferous trees
2 Utility
3 Workshop
4 Bedroom zone
5 Office zone
6 Master bedroom zone
7 Living area
8 Dining area
9 Wood stove
10 Kitchen
11 Entry/storage
12 Deciduous trees

4

6

5

4 Site plan
5 Dining room and kitchen from solar gallery
6 Solar gallery
7 Living and dining rooms
8 Dining room, kitchen and solar gallery
9 Living room with 'heat sink' stone wall
10 Bathroom

Photography: Philip Castleton

7

8

9

10

IA HOUSE

VALLE DE BRAVO, MEXICO

BGP ARQUITECTURA

The IA House sits on a slope on the outskirts of Valle de Bravo with a view overlooking the lake. The remains of stone walls, previously covered by soil and gravel, were discovered on the site. It was decided that they would be kept and a crystal prism placed over them. The height of these wall remains defined the levels of the project.

A series of fringes, parallel to the lake and perpendicular to the slope of the site, delineate the different platforms of the interior as well as the exterior spaces. The crystal volume is suspended in a kind of fragile equilibrium between two bodies of water: the lap pool and the lake. The crystal volume, with its Cartesian clarity and strict order, organises the program structure and comprises the living room, dining room and main bedroom, which are all separated by a low volume that houses the service areas. The prism, simultaneously transparent and translucent, is placed over a stone basement that holds two bedrooms.

The wooden roof supported by thin columns seems to float over the interior walls without touching them, achieving spatial continuity. Its inclined plane responds to local urban guidelines and is tilted to the north, opening itself to the view, its overhang filtering the sun. This wooden pergola extends the plane towards the outside in the same way that the internal floor extends towards the patio, expanding the interior space and blurring the boundaries between interior and exterior. Materials have been kept to a minimum, using a neutral palette that enhances the colours of the lake, mountains and sky and emphasises changes in vegetation and landscape.

The glazed envelope, besides displaying a continuous view, creates a play of transparency and opaqueness that varies throughout the day. The joins between materials reveal the construction system and its structural logic - the relationships between the materials that complement and reinforce the building.

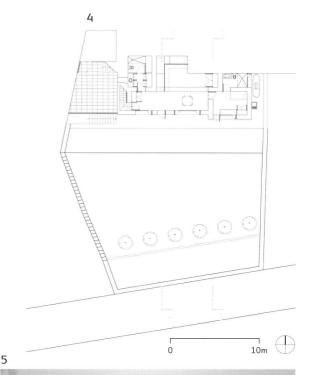

1   Façade from the lake
2   Living room with view to the lake
3   View from the pool to the living room
4   Main floor plan
5   Children's bedroom
6   Pool area

Photography: Luis Gordoa

INDIAN NECK RESIDENCE

WELLFLEET, CAPE COD, MASSACHUSETTS, USA

HAMMER ARCHITECTS

This new four-bedroom home is situated on a heavily wooded hillside overlooking a tidal marsh. The house is informed by the tradition of modern residential architecture that prevailed on this portion of Cape Cod in the mid 20th century. It has been designed to visually connect interior and exterior living spaces, to provide ample natural light and ventilation and to carefully integrate the built environment with the landscape. The home is nestled into the hill and oriented to maximise views on the water side.

Natural ventilation was the critical sustainable-design concern as the house is occupied primarily during the summer months. To eliminate the need for air-conditioning and reduce energy consumption, the afternoon sun is shielded on the southwest façade by the overhanging roof, while the large view windows on the opposite side are oriented to permit ample ventilation and daylight and to minimise solar gain. The sloped ceiling of the main living space directs warm air to several sets of high, motorised awning windows. These windows are protected from rain by the overhang, allowing their continuous use, even in inclement weather.

A linear metal canopy delineates the entrance. It is detailed as an attachment to a wall and is physically separated from the main volume of the house by tall vertical windows. This layering element encloses the main staircase and entry hall and is distinguished by its board-formed concrete foundation and horizontal tongue-and-groove cedar siding. The upper floor, which is level with grade on the entry side, contains the living and dining rooms, kitchen and master bedroom. The living room wing is distinctly articulated from the master bedroom wing by its higher volume, clerestory strip windows and large patio doors opening onto the deck and terrace. The lower level has three walkout bedrooms on the waterside, each with a private deck.

The red cedar clapboards, tongue-and-groove siding and trim have been finished with a clear stain. The metal fascias at the roof and canopy enhance the transition between the building and the sky. Simple volumes, expansive glass walls and exposed wood structural beams and roof decking characterise the interiors. Floors are European steamed beech, linoleum, slate and quarry tile.

1

2

4

3

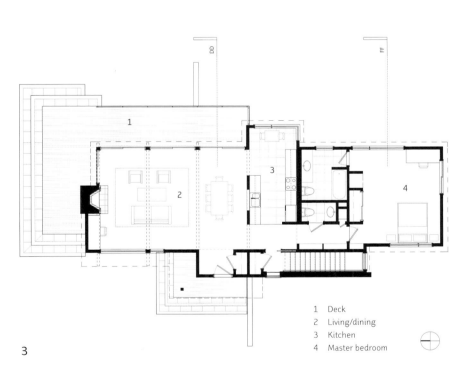

1   Deck
2   Living/dining
3   Kitchen
4   Master bedroom

1   Elevation facing tidal marsh
2   Stair to lower level
3   Upper level plan
4   Living room looking north
5   Dining room

Photography: Bill Lyons

5

JACKALOPE RANCH

DRIPPING SPRING, TEXAS, USA

TROUT STUDIOS

On 2.5 secluded hectares beside the Pedernales River in Texas Hill Country, Jackalope Ranch encompasses the 315-square-metre single-family residence of designer Sallie Trout and husband Geoff Cline as well as Trout's 170-square-metre artist studio/wood and metal shop. The new multi-level structure is a low-impact green building with environmental innovations including a rainwater collection and filtration system that supplies all water for the site. Sheathed in galvalume-skinned metal SIPs and salvaged local cypress, the unpainted exterior blends into the rustic surroundings. The solid mahogany main door faces northwest while the main living space opens to 90 metres of river frontage facing southeast – next to it is an outdoor living room created from a cypress-clad frame that was part of the previous residence. A tranquil, dark-bottomed, solar-heated lap pool sits between the house and a glade of oak trees.

Designed with Trout's signature mix of playfulness, sophistication and functionality, the house's main interior space is an expansive great room merging living, dining and kitchen areas. A central library tower is as dramatic a flight of the imagination as it is a soaring vertical space. The most frequently used books are on the lower shelves, and a boatswain's chair on an engine-powered chain hoist accesses additional volumes at elevations up to 12 metres. A ground-floor guest suite with rolling cabinets and a pitched ceiling doubles as a recording studio; a home office has his-and-hers workstations on a 'floating' desk of solid pecan. The master suite on the second level displays favourites from Cline's guitar collection in the bedroom, and a sitting area integrates scenic views and a cosy fireplace. A third-floor screened porch with windows all around invites breezes even on the hottest afternoon. Trout-designed furniture and accessories enliven the entire house, which is wired for CAD 5 computer/communications, making it a fully contained live–work retreat.

1   *View towards artist's studio and wood/metal shop*

2   *Solar-heated lap pool*

3   *Outdoor living room*

1	Entry
2	Living room
3	Dining room
4	Kitchen
5	Pantry
6	Laundry
7	Office
8	Guest bedroom
9	Bathroom

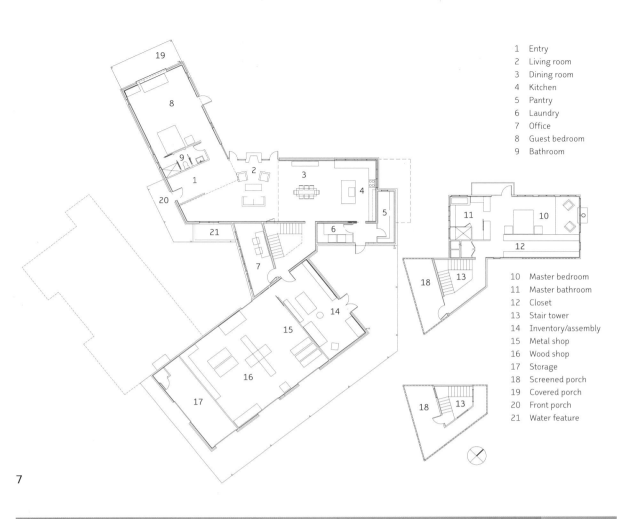

10	Master bedroom
11	Master bathroom
12	Closet
13	Stair tower
14	Inventory/assembly
15	Metal shop
16	Wood shop
17	Storage
18	Screened porch
19	Covered porch
20	Front porch
21	Water feature

7

9

8

4 *Elevated seating area in master bedroom*

5 *Open kitchen/dining area*

6 *Master bathroom entry*

7 *Floor plans*

8 *Master bedroom*

9 *Kitchen island*

Photography: Hardaway & Hester

1   *Looking south through dining and kitchen*
2   *From court to Cape Volnay; outside, inside, outside*
3   *Reflecting the afternoon sun, the house is set discreetly in the vast landscape*
4   *Rammed earth, glass and steel frame the landscape*
5   *Floor plan*

Photography: Earl Carter

JOHANNA HOUSE

JOHANNA, VICTORIA, AUSTRALIA

NICHOLAS BURNS ASSOCIATES

The Johanna House is a journey of landscape, ocean and detailed, considered design. Juxtapositions of contraction and expansion, opacity and transparency, and structure and wilderness create a balance capable of distorting the experience of time and place.

Just west of Cape Otway in southwestern Victoria, an old country track leads from the Great Ocean Road to a simple farm gate in a cathedral of pristine, native forest. Beyond the gate, a 1-kilometre track snakes through the 40-hectare property of protected wilderness that is home to endangered flora and fauna. The hypnotic forest gently quietens your mind, covertly preparing you for the experience of the Johanna House.

The house is sited on an existing clearing; no trees were felled for construction. To further protect the property's flora and fauna, as well as that of the adjoining national park, no outside material was brought onto the site, preventing the invasion of non-indigenous species.

A discreet addition to the landscape, the house is a journey of gradual and layered concealment that opens up to the natural surroundings and ocean views. Pure geometry, a limited material palette and careful detailing combine to create a feeling of stillness – a dematerialising interconnection with nature, landscape and time.

At first glimpse, a weightless flat roof waits behind a rammed-earth wall – seemingly providing a threshold between the life left behind and the new consciousness of the house. This wall, a concentration of local earth, leads to a partially open entrance hall, which initially conceals the expanse of the surrounding landscape. A glass front door provides entry to the house, and leads to another turn in the journey, further heightening the senses. At the edge of the freestanding wall situated directly inside the door, the ocean's full expanse is finally revealed.

Tanks collect rainwater for drinking, household use and fire-fighting requirements. Wastewater is treated onsite using biological aerobic sand filtration that requires no chemical or power input.

1

2

3

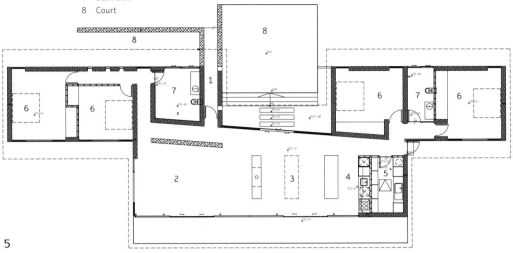

1 Entrance
2 Living room
3 Dining room
4 Kitchen
5 Store/laundry
6 Bedroom
7 Bathroom
8 Court

5

4

KANGAROO VALLEY HOUSE

KANGAROO VALLEY, NEW SOUTH WALES, AUSTRALIA

TURNER + ASSOCIATES

The Kangaroo Valley House is sited on a cleared plateau near the edge of an escarpment and surrounded by rugged bushland. The long meandering approach means that the house is gradually revealed.

The house consists of a family of containers - roofed and open to the sky. A selection of materials including concrete, copper and timber have been assigned to the three key elements of the house: the living volume, the garage and southern courtyard enclosure, and the usable outdoor ground planes. Concrete is used in instances where connections to the ground are made. Copper is used as a crafted, soft surface - its patina makes a connection with the red-brown eucalypt leaves on the ground and the purple-brown hues of the tall bloodwoods and stringybarks that dominate the site. Timber is used on the external living surfaces as a rich but domestic contrast to the cladding and structural materials.

The geometry of the house is simple and orthogonal, forming quietly arranged spaces within the dramatic natural landscape. The first container accommodates the primary interior living spaces, which run east–west, and is wrapped in copper. It cantilevers 4.5 metres to the east making a generous undercroft arrival space along with an extension of the copper wall cladding that wraps down and underneath to line this and other projections. This element is elevated on a concrete second container accommodating entry lobby, parking garage, workshop and utility areas. This lower space diminishes from a fully visible level on the east side to meet the adjacent rising ground level towards the west. To the south of the primary living space is the third container, an open-air room with outdoor fireplace. It is enclosed on three sides by 2.4-metre-high concrete walls with openings that frame local views and shield the house from southwesterly winds and by night expose the intensity of a sky never seen in the city.

The 7.5- by 28-metre living volume has an ironbark-lined verandah to the north that appears carved from the copper container. This space is oriented north towards the valley, river and mountain range and during the summer months it provides deep protection from the sun. Operable external shading devices screen secondary bedrooms and a studio at the northwest end of the house.

Opposite   The interlocking concrete and copper forms within the bush setting

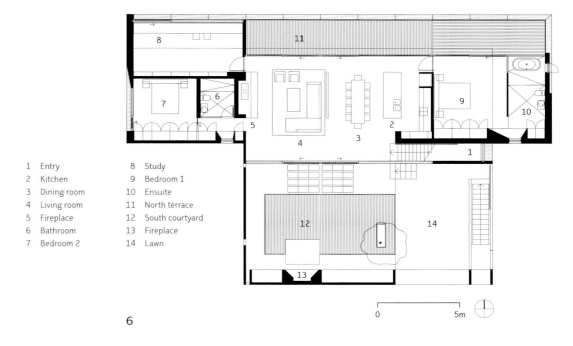

1	Entry	8	Study
2	Kitchen	9	Bedroom 1
3	Dining room	10	Ensuite
4	Living room	11	North terrace
5	Fireplace	12	South courtyard
6	Bathroom	13	Fireplace
7	Bedroom 2	14	Lawn

0   5m

6

5

2   The interior opens out to both courtyard and bush

3   The living space and dining area are divided by a
     floating screen

4   Study space with retractable blinds

5   The long, timber-lined balcony unites the interior
     spaces

6   Floor plan

Photography: Shannon McGrath (1); Brett Boardman (2,3,4,5)

KILMORE HOUSE

KILMORE, VICTORIA, AUSTRALIA

INTERMODE WITH CARR DESIGN GROUP

The 850-square-metre Kilmore House is situated on a 200-hectare property, 60 kilometres north of Melbourne. The house sits within a paddock previously burnt out by a bushfire. The area is defined by a cluster of burnt tree trunks to the south and views to the property's dam to the north. Surrounded by green country landscape and pasture for Black Angus cattle, the five-bedroom, three-bathroom house enjoys magnificent views and access to the outside from every room via floor-to-ceiling sliding glass doors.

Embracing the philosophy of the modular approach, the house was built over two structures. The main house includes living, dining, kitchen, study, separate laundry, cool room, bedrooms and bathrooms. The entertaining zone is separated from the sleeping zones and again from the master bedroom and ensuite wing by glazed walkways. The guest pavilion, connected to the main house by decking, includes another living area and kitchenette, along with additional guest bedrooms and a bathroom. A custom four-car carport was designed in keeping with the rest of the home.

The pavilions were conceived as freestanding elements, darkly clad, to sit as objects within the stark surrounding landscape. The notion of the pavilion was used to create semi-enclosed external decked areas that provide protection from harsh winds while defining view lines.

Exploring the notion of the pavilions as stand-alone objects, the house forgoes the typical notion of 'front and rear' – instead the pavilions and decking are used to define seasonal areas of dark thoughtful spaces for the cooler months, protected from the elements, as well as light areas for the warmer months to maximise connection with outdoor areas and the cooling breezes.

1

2

3

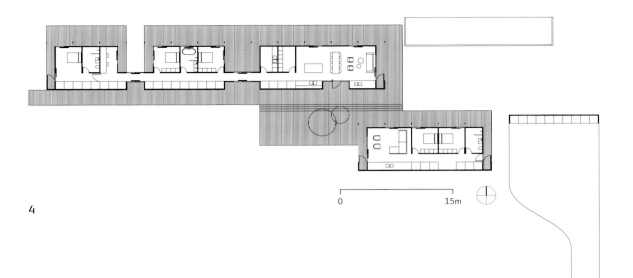

4

Photography: Derek Swalwell

6

9

7

8

KNOCKFAD HOUSE

KNOCKFAD, BALLYHAISE, COUNTY CAVAN, IRELAND

DAMIEN MURTAGH ARCHITECTS

The Knockfad House's evolution was in direct response to its site, the client's brief and its rural setting. Damien Murtagh Architects was asked to design a house for modern living that would take advantage of its raised rural setting while always remaining sympathetic to its environment and the local architecture. For this reason a blend of traditional building forms together with subtle modern interventions were adopted, lending an understated feel to this sensitive project.

The layout of the building is defined by three distinct cores: the sleeping, circulation and living quarters. On approach to the house a long linear stone façade structure is broken only by the soft white lines of the juxtaposed oval form of the garage. This area accommodates the east sleeping quarters, while also providing a sound and privacy barrier to the rest of the house from the country road.

The central circulation core, which primarily acts as a buffer zone between living and sleeping areas, has a number of additional functions. These include a greeting hall on the upper level and a library/study, which has both views and access to a tranquil garden through a large expanse of glazing, on the lower level.

The rear living core has been offset and has a 10-metre opening to take full advantage of the vast, beautiful rural landscape beyond. The kitchen/dining area is connected to the living room through a large sliding-screen wall. The ceiling form is exposed here and can be seen to run through to the living room by way of frameless glass at clerestory level above the sliding wall. The exposed ceiling continues into the sitting room, which is accessed down a series of steps within the circulation core, giving it additional height. A sizeable corner glazing element provides spectacular views of six counties in the distance.

The harmonious synthesis of local stone, render, pre-aged copper, mahogany and natural slate forms a most positive rural intervention. The Knockfad House is a highly energy-efficient A-rated dwelling, with a wood-pellet burner, solar panelling and Kingspan rigid insulation installed throughout.

Opposite   North face in late evening

2

3

4

5

6

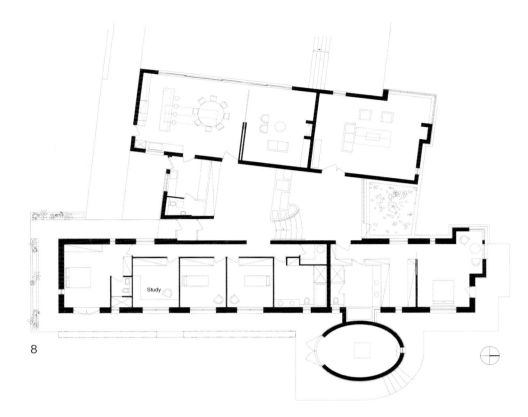

8

7

2   Linear stone
3   Corner glazing and fireplace
4   Master bedroom
5   Walnut library bookcase
6   View from library
7   Country kitchen
8   Ground floor plan

Photography: Anthony Hopkins and Dennis Gilbert

Study

KOHLHAGEN RESIDENCE

SOUTHERN COLORADO, USA

4240 ARCHITECTURE

The Kohlhagen Residence overlooks the San Juan Mountains in Southern Colorado. The breathtaking views of the Navajo and Banded Peaks to the east, Pagosa Peak to the north, and an aspen-filled valley to the west provide the perfect setting for this western dream retreat. Two guest cabins act as gateways to the site, each designed to respond to site-specific views and microenvironments on this 60-hectare ranch preserve.

Conceived for two writers, and accompanied by guest homes for their adult sons, the main house is designed on a simple linear plan, aligned on the north axis. The interior spaces foster the owners' personalities by alternating their love of light and desire for darkness. The dark, intimate spaces open up to dynamic, light-filled spaces – providing inspiration for the two writers.

Warm stone, plaster, hand-finished woods, and custom-designed iron fixtures bring texture to the interiors that express the client's Northern New Mexico aesthetic. The house, constructed of plaster walls and a Galvalume zinc roof, with all major spaces opening directly to the exterior, provides daylong access to the movement of the sun.

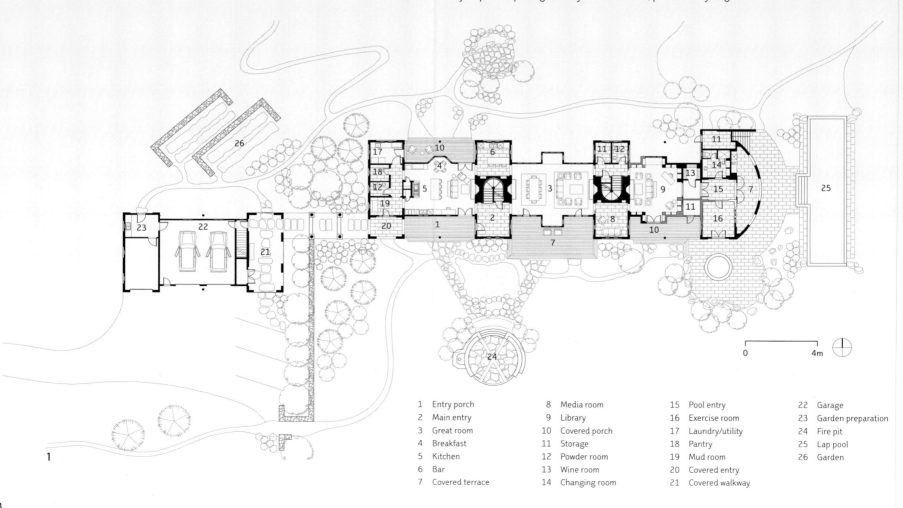

1	Entry porch	8	Media room	15	Pool entry	22	Garage
2	Main entry	9	Library	16	Exercise room	23	Garden preparation
3	Great room	10	Covered porch	17	Laundry/utility	24	Fire pit
4	Breakfast	11	Storage	18	Pantry	25	Lap pool
5	Kitchen	12	Powder room	19	Mud room	26	Garden
6	Bar	13	Wine room	20	Covered entry		
7	Covered terrace	14	Changing room	21	Covered walkway		

2

3

4

1   Ground floor plan
2   Main residence at night
3   Outdoor living room landscape
4   Two-storey great room

Photography: Frank Ooms Photography

KURREKI

Kurreki is a purpose-built retreat in the tiny village of Seal Rocks on the North Coast of New South Wales. Surrounded by both the Myall Lakes National Park and the Great Lakes Marine Park, Kurreki offers welcome respite from the increasingly urbanised sprawl of the cities.

The design is intentionally a cross between camping and luxury accommodation and employs strategies designed to allow inhabitants to relax and unwind. All spaces open to the outside, resulting in a connectedness with the natural elements.

The building has a tough exterior to provide privacy, bushfire protection and a sense of solitude. Spaces encircle a central deck and garden, with all rooms opening up one wall to the central space. Rather than glass and fly screens for the bedrooms there are roller shutters and mosquito nets that offer the feel of camping. An added benefit is the sky view created by establishing a circular perimeter.

Bathing facilities are stripped back to the bare essentials: a single toilet in fibre cement partitioning and a huge double shower that can open to the deck with just a curtain or be closed off for total privacy.

The home is also low impact: a worm farm treats sewer waste onsite, all water is collected from the roof and a variety of other water and energy saving devices are employed.

Materials throughout are honest and serviceable. External cladding is unpainted compressed cement sheet. Roller shutters are plain zincalume, joinery is concrete formply left unfinished. To counter the harsh exterior, Murobond colours are used extensively inside to enliven the spaces and provide a link to the colours of nature.

Opposite   View across courtyard towards living room

2

2   Living room with daybed
3   Kitchen opening onto deck
4   Floor plan
5   View from rear, looking through hammock deck
6   Bathroom

Photography: Simon Whitbread

3

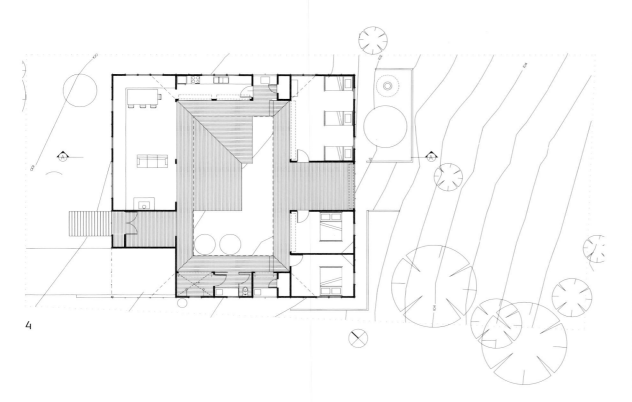

4

6

5

LIVERMORE HOUSE

MONTEREY, CALIFORNIA, USA

MOORE RUBLE YUDELL ARCHITECTS AND PLANNERS

Santa Lucia Preserve is a spectacular 7300-hectare ecological preserve that has remained relatively untouched since the time of the early California Ranchos. The land has been planned to protect and preserve an extraordinarily diverse range of classic California landscapes from oak knolls, to riparian corridors and redwood groves.

The owners became enamoured with the diversity and beauty of the preserve's ecology and the serenity of its environment. They selected a site where gentle hills and valleys provide a sense of protection. This intimacy is complemented by the dramatic vistas of distant mountains. The family is energetic, with interests as diverse as cutting-edge technology, photography and the natural environment. They wanted a house that could accommodate a broad range of family and individual activities.

The house evolved in close response to the landscape, creating diverse settings for family and individuals. The crescent shape of the main residence reflects the undulations of the topography. It preserves the knoll and optimises views south to distant California coastal ranges and north to adjacent ridgelines.

Moore Ruble Yudell, in collaboration with Audrey Alberts Interior Design, conceived a house organised as a series of carefully proportioned rooms, which are linked by an arcing gallery that provides a constantly changing perspective into the landscape. Major rooms are spatially extended by their adjacency to the gallery. A series of intimate courtyards are interleaved between these rooms creating additional exposures to landscape, light and breezes. Gently terraced stairways and generous bays further enhance the choreography of habitation.

A sweeping zinc roof reflects the changing colours of the sky and provides southern shade while rising to receive the gentle northern daylight. The colours and materials of the house were selected based on careful study of the rocks, soil and native vegetation. They respond to the changing light in ways that reinforce the connection to the land and the cycles of nature. The buildings, their inhabitants and the environment are united in a harmonious yet dynamic relationship.

Opposite   North elevation of the main house

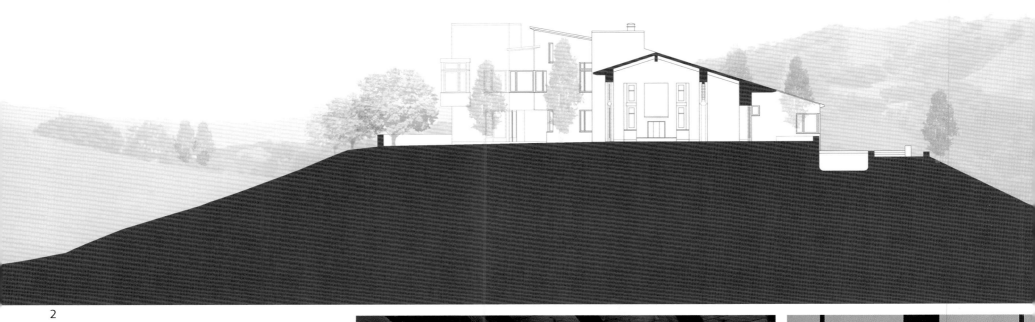

2

2   Site section
3   Master bedroom
4   View of living area in the great room of the main house
5   Dining area in the great room of the main house

Photography: David O Marlow

3

4

LORD RESIDENCE

ASPEN, COLORADO, USA

STUDIO B ARCHITECTS

This flat half-hectare site is close to the City of Aspen and has spectacular views to the nearby ski slopes and Pyramid Peak. The 836-square-metre project is ordered by a 56-centimetre-thick rammed-earth wall, which serves as a buffer against noise from the neighbouring highway.

This earthen wall is composed of sifted soil from the site that was mixed with concrete and poured in 'lifts' providing the horizontal striations. It has a wonderful texture and patina and offers the element of contrast to the more refined interior surfaces. The exterior surfaces are composed of rusted vertical steel panels, Kalwall translucent panels, aluminium windows and doors, zinc roofing and flashing with the textured earth wall.

The main level program, separated into a public zone and master and children's wing, was restricted to a single storey so as not to obstruct views. The entire main level revolves around and protects the large south-facing terrace and landscape. The sloping roof forms drain away from the terraces and open the interiors to views and sunshine.

The adjacent highway noise, single-storey limitation and south-facing orientation provided challenges for this project and the site had sat vacant for some time prior to the owners purchasing the property. An elaborate glazing system and window treatments address the intense Colorado sun. The site allowed the main level plan to branch out, yielding the low profile, and the thick wall with few openings facing the highway keeps the noise to a minimum.

Opposite   The low profile of the architecture allows it to integrate with its surroundings

2

3

4

2 View to south courtyard and Aspen Mountain

3 Front entry integrates rusted metal panels, rammed earth and translucent panels

4 View from courtyard over reflecting pool into interior living space

5 Master bedroom

6 The exterior courtyard is an extension of the interior spaces

7 Main level floor plan

8 View of the kitchen area

Photography: Paul Warchol (1,4,5,8); Aspen Architectural Photography (2,3,6)

5

7

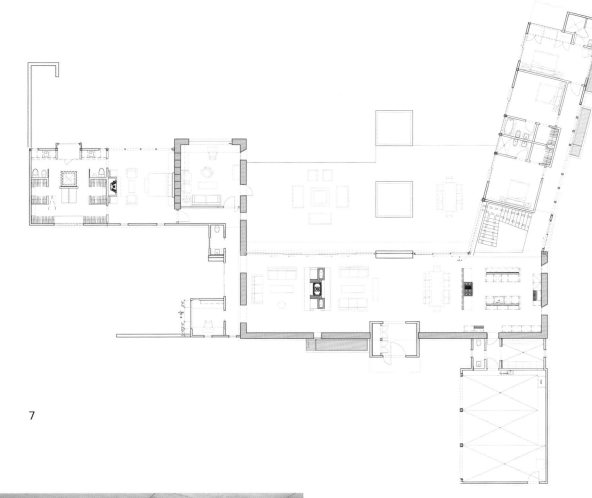

6

8

MACEDON COURTYARD HOUSE

MACEDON, VICTORIA, AUSTRALIA

ZEN ARCHITECTS

The Macedon house was designed to be an environmentally sensitive building that would endure the passing of time. A minimum 100-year life span was envisaged for the house in a climate that includes frosts, snow, extreme heat and bushfires.

Local limestone is used externally for its ability to withstand the elements and internally for its thermal mass. The limestone was carved and laid by an experienced team of stonemasons. Unconstrained by the tight timelines governing most projects, the house evolved slowly, allowing the architecture to express the quality of the workmanship.

The courtyard plan allows for passive solar gain and enhances passive cooling through cross ventilation as the water feature and the courtyard landscape cool the breezes.

Rooms are placed specifically according to the contours of the land, views and orientation to the sun. The living wing is located on the south of the courtyard and enjoys panoramic views to the south while gaining sunlight via the courtyard to the north. A writer's studio is on the west side of the courtyard while the bedroom wing projects towards the east.

Technology is used to allow the house to actively harness elements. Heating is provided by a solar powered hydronic system within the floor. Windows open automatically when required to catch prevailing breezes and close automatically in the case of bushfires.

The house offers many ecologically sustainable design features including a courtyard designed to maximise passive solar gain for natural heating in winter and promote natural cooling through cross ventilation in summer, solar hot water integrated with a hydronic heating system in the insulated ground floor concrete slab and a worm farm sewerage treatment system. Additionally, the pool is used as a 'heat sink' to dump excess heat generated by the solar system, rainwater is harvested and stored in tanks, stormwater from the site is collected and retained in dams, and summer heat is naturally removed by a two-storey stair void acting as a thermal chimney.

1   Courtyard looking west to the writing studio and library
2   Floor plans
3   Western view over small dam
4   Kitchen, dining and living room
5   Writing studio and library

Photography: Emma Cross

1

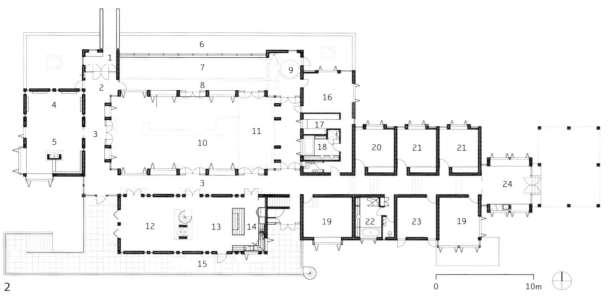

2

1	Porch	13	Dining
2	Formal entry	14	Kitchen
3	Link	15	Terrace
4	Writer's office	16	Master bedroom
5	Library	17	Walk-in robe
6	Pond	18	Ensuite
7	Lap pool	19	Office
8	Pool pavilion	20	Guest bedroom
9	Spa	21	Bedroom
10	Courtyard	22	Bathroom
11	Courtyard terrace	23	Media room
12	Living	24	Laundry

0   10m

3

4

5

MARTINBOROUGH HOUSE

MARTINBOROUGH, WAIRARAPA, NEW ZEALAND

PARSONSON ARCHITECTS

This 400-square-metre house is located in a semi-rural area on the east side of Martinborough, a one-hour drive north of Wellington, on New Zealand's North Island. It is surrounded by plantations of olives and grapes, pastureland and rolling hills. The brief was to create a house that engaged with its surroundings by allowing the landscape to flow up and into the house.

On approach, a rurally inspired corrugated-iron wall 'runs away' and turns 90 degrees to contain the arrival space. The main roof glides over this, leading into the house. Entry is into a gallery space (the owners are keen art collectors) and the house opens out to the property from here, addressing sunlight and views.

The design was generated from the idea of linking lines from the house out into the landscape and vice versa (the lines of vegetation will soon be planted). The house sits long and low in this large, multilayered landscape and, as such, quietly slips into it. The dark corrugated-iron walls are in tune with the dark lines of the macrocarpa planting in the distance.

The boundary between inside and outside is blurred by the continuity of floors and terraces and the roofs that hover or glide lightly across the plan. The plan slips loosely from one space to another as it moves across the land. To the west, the composition is pinned to the ground by the living areas' three large fireplaces.

1   View towards the house and hills

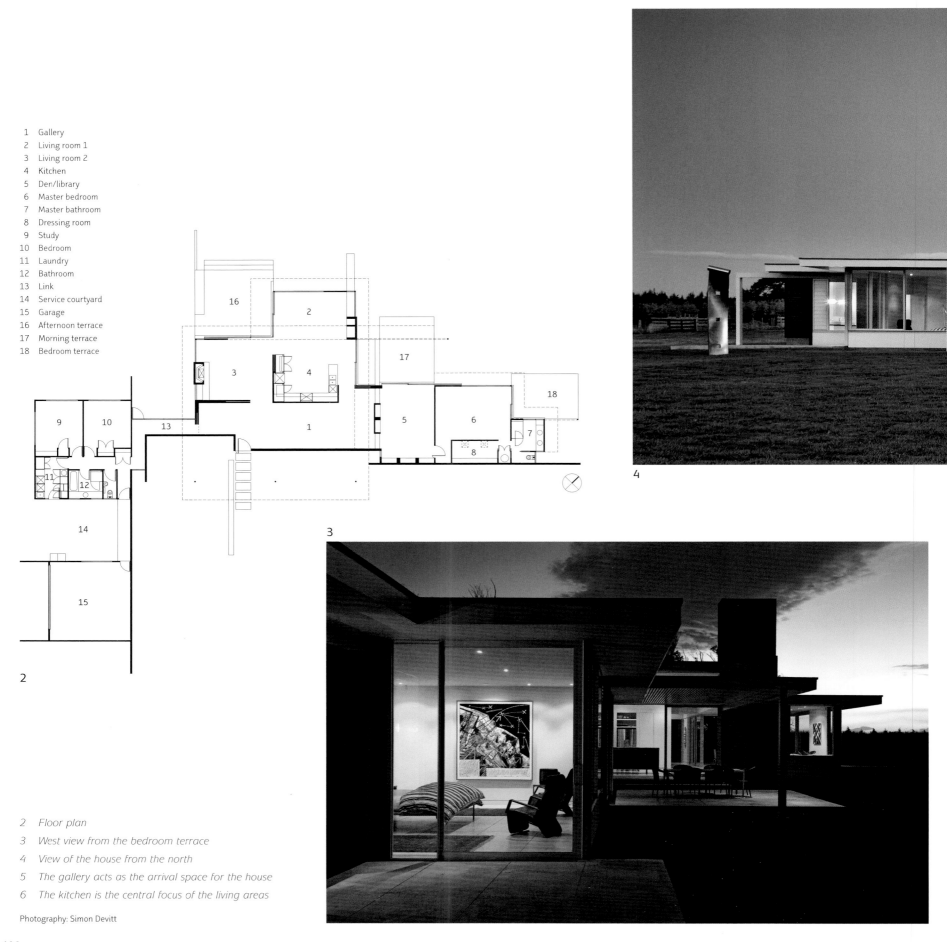

1 Gallery
2 Living room 1
3 Living room 2
4 Kitchen
5 Den/library
6 Master bedroom
7 Master bathroom
8 Dressing room
9 Study
10 Bedroom
11 Laundry
12 Bathroom
13 Link
14 Service courtyard
15 Garage
16 Afternoon terrace
17 Morning terrace
18 Bedroom terrace

2   Floor plan
3   West view from the bedroom terrace
4   View of the house from the north
5   The gallery acts as the arrival space for the house
6   The kitchen is the central focus of the living areas

Photography: Simon Devitt

196

5

6

MOLLY'S CABIN

POINTE AU BARIL, ONTARIO, CANADA

AGATHOM CO.

Three and a half hours north of Toronto is Pointe au Baril, a remote archipelago in Georgian Bay on a cusp of the Canadian Shield – a large area of exposed Precambrian rock. Twelve kilometres from the marina on a 1-hectare island is Molly's Cabin, a private seasonal retreat for a multi-generational family. The aim of the project was to balance comfort with the bare necessities so that its inhabitants live lightly on the land and fully engage with their surroundings.

The 93-square-metre cabin consists of a bedroom, a living room with a library nook, a kitchen/dining room and a small loft that can serve as a drawing studio, library, playroom or supplementary bedroom. Although open in plan, the L-shaped design facilitates both privacy and interaction. Wooden decks and bridges extend the interior to the outdoors. While modernist architectural ideals are at work, the design is a playful reinterpretation of the humble architectural vernacular found on these islands. The cabin fits snugly against the boulders and is sited close to the edge of the water. Shielded behind a large rock and a signature tree, there are multiple views of the fast-changing weather from under the shelter of the tent-like flaps.

Topped by a broad shingled asphalt roof and constructed from recovered timbers, the cabin is anchored by a Rumford fireplace that makes use of local stone. The building is designed with plenty of dual-function elements: exposed rafters provide additional storage, a dining-room cabinet doubles as an outdoor tool shed and the library windows roll open to convert the interior into a breezeway. Solar panels power a pump that draws fresh water from the lake. Fuel for the stove, fridge and lamps is supplied by propane or lamp oil. On the other side of the island there is an outhouse with a composting toilet and two older sleeping bunks.

Molly's Cabin is familiar, experimental, respectful and assertive. The design challenges the current tendency in the area for extravagant architectural statements, creating a solution that is inventive and sustainable.

1   View from east looking towards open water
2   Floor plan
3   The western view to open water
4   View of living room and library with dining room beyond

Photography: Paul Orenstein and Michael Awad

1

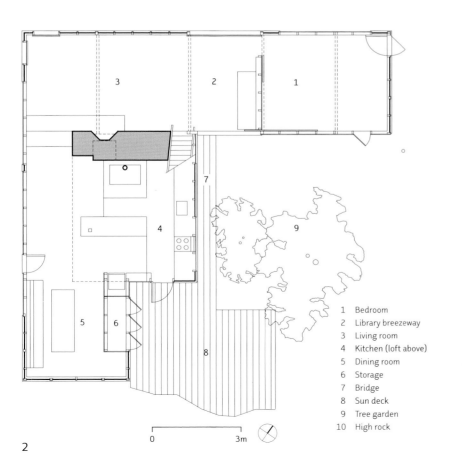

2

3

4

10

3   2   1

7

4   9

5   6

8

1   Bedroom
2   Library breezeway
3   Living room
4   Kitchen (loft above)
5   Dining room
6   Storage
7   Bridge
8   Sun deck
9   Tree garden
10   High rock

0   3m

MOUNT TAURUS RESIDENCE

COLD SPRING, NEW YORK, USA

ZIVKOVIC CONNOLLY ARCHITECTS

This new country house is sited on 6 hectares of hillside and looks out over the treetops of adjacent reserve lands and beyond to the majestic Hudson River and high stone walls of the West Point Military Academy.

The house enjoys an easy and flowing spatial relationship between indoor and outdoor areas and takes full advantage of the splendid panoramic view. Doors and windows align in plan wherever possible and are generously sized to optimise the view and to conveniently integrate indoor and outdoor living. Internally, the systems and services are all state-of-the-art and sensitively submissive to the architectural detail.

The design is characterised by a symmetrical stone block with an elemental quality reinforced by four square, chimney-like and symmetrically placed towers. These towers conceal unsightly flues and mechanical items as well the elevator and stair access to the rooftop widow's walk, contributing to the building's Palladian simplicity of form. The same stone that defines the house is used in the retaining walls, which add to the fortified appearance of the compound and simultaneously establish the terrace levels. The house appears to emerge naturally out of the stony ground of the site. The selection of stone was inspired by the local West Point aesthetic of dominant granite fields and limestone detail and the articulation of the exterior is focused on the detailing of the stonework, including stringcourse, quoining and trimming of openings.

Local seismic activity and the house's steep and stony site on the southern face of Mount Taurus presented challenges with respect to indoor–outdoor planning, vehicular access, design of building foundations, stormwater drainage and sewage disposal. The solution incorporated a sequence of three principal terraces that step down the hillside and accommodate, in descending order, the arrival court, the house and the main outdoor recreational area with a pool. The reinforced-concrete walls retaining the terraces are granite-faced and continuous with deep raft slabs that anchor the foundations and resist lateral forces. Stormwater is diverted to natural drainage channels and sewage is directed down the site to a septic field.

While the characteristic materials and overall architectural form of the Mount Taurus Residence are timeless, the planning, detailing and technology define an ensemble that is altogether modern.

Opposite   South façade has views towards the Hudson River Valley

2 Arrival court

3 Ground floor plan

4 West dining terrace with breezeway and garage building
   beyond

5 Entrance hall and view through living room to Hudson
   River Valley beyond

6 South-facing façade and swimming pool

7 Living room looking north towards entrance hall beyond

Photography: Jonathan Wallen

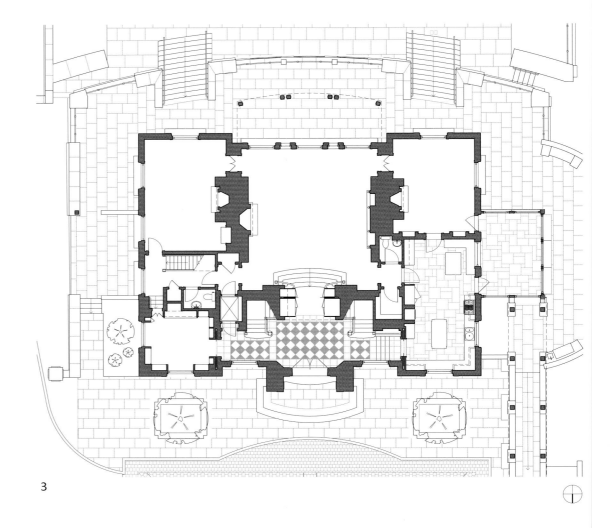

3

2

4

5

7

6

MOUNTAIN STAR II
RESIDENCE

AVON, COLORADO, USA

4240 ARCHITECTURE

Overlooking Vail Valley and the Gore Range at 2500 metres, this 1-hectare, dramatically sloped and heavily wooded site presented physical, environmental and political challenges, but also glorious opportunities for drama and seclusion, spectacular views and filtered sunlight.

The owners asked the architects to develop a modest compound for family gatherings – a getaway from their busy professional lives – that would combine both their love of the simplicity of rural Italy and the excitement of their city penthouse.

The home is organised into three 7-metre-deep stone 'cottages', all detailed in a similar manner and joined by two steel and glass greenhouses, one of which opens onto a stone-paved porch that links the guest parking and garage to the entryway. The other is a dramatic two-storey transparent space connected by bridges to the solid stone side walls of the adjacent cottages.

The uppermost cottage contains the garages, storage for bikes, skis and snowshoes and the entry/mudroom. This cottage is aligned with the site contours to reduce the side hill excavation and provide an auto-court arrival that remains sun-filled during the heavy snowfall of the mountain seasons. The other two cottages are aligned across the arc of the contours to capture the 180-degree views of New York Mountain and Mount Jackson.

The middle cottage, designed as an informal loft-like space, has an entrance galleria overlooking a lower great room/dining area that in turn overlooks a still-lower kitchen/family area. Stone floors give way to walnut wood floors; plastered walls define the northern interior elevations, glass window walls open to the south, while stone walls with fireplaces define the east and west walls.

The third cottage contains the master suite on the upper level, which opens onto its own outside covered porch offering spectacular views. Three guest suites occupy the lower level. A steel-framed stair leads to this lower level and a private screening room that opens to a secluded stone-surrounded hot tub set in the forest meadow.

Copper-shingled roofs, a rich ox-blood stained wood siding and windows clad with bronze metal complete the palette of materials. The horizontal alignments of the window systems act as a counterpart to the verticality of the surrounding aspens. Walnut doors and floors, plastered walls and ceilings and nickel hardware are the framework materials for a minimal interior setting. According to the owners, 'To live here is to live in a work of art.'

1   South outdoor living space
2   View from south of master bedroom and living spaces
3   View from northeast through aspen grove

1

3

2

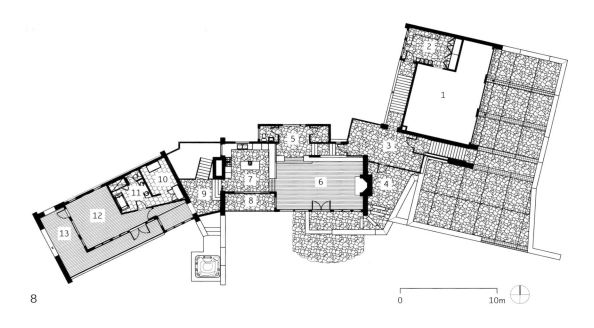

8

0   10m

1 Garage	11 Master bathroom
2 Mud room	12 Master bedroom
3 Entry	13 Master terrace
4 East terrace	14 Hot tub terrace
5 Entry hall	15 Laundry
6 Living/dining room	16 Guest bedroom
7 Kitchen	17 Lower west terrace
8 Patio	18 Theatre entry
9 Upper west terrace	19 Home theatre
10 Master closet	

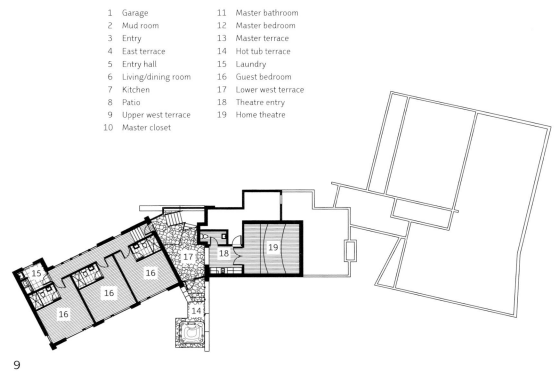

9

4   *View from entry hall*

5   *Master bedroom*

6   *Interior view from kitchen to living room*

7   *Living room*

8   *Upper level floor plan*

9   *Lower level floor plan*

Photography: David Marlow

THE PATON HOUSE

RUAKAKA, NEW ZEALAND

STUDIO JOHN IRVING

The Paton House is a busy working farmhouse for a successful family with four children. Progressive young farmers with the awards to prove it, the owners knew that a brick and tile suburban solution wasn't for them. Because this was John Irving's first New Zealand project after almost 10 years in Europe he was determined to keep it simple, regional and in line with the clients' budget.

The site is on a windswept hill overlooking a dairy farm, the speedy straights of Ruakaka's State Highway One and the distant sea views of the Whangarei Heads and the Hen and Chicks Islands. It's a spectacular view. The design responds to this as three separate blocks for sleeping, living and working (with its own separate farm entry). The blocks are linked by a concrete spine that runs the length of the house and conceptually braces it from the howling westerly winds. The gaps between the blocks form sheltered courtyards. The spine's other purpose is separating the open sloping roofed pavilion front from the closed back, which forms the entry area and arrival court. Oriented to the northeast, the house suits this family of early risers. The house also doubles as their new bach (the old one being sold to pay for it) so the detailing is casual: finger pulls on plywood doors, sliding doors hiding secret laundry and storage rooms and the television is also hidden away. The house provides a backdrop to the theatre of this family's daily life, and will adapt well to their changing needs.

1

1 The farm entry
2 The three linked pavilions
3 Family room

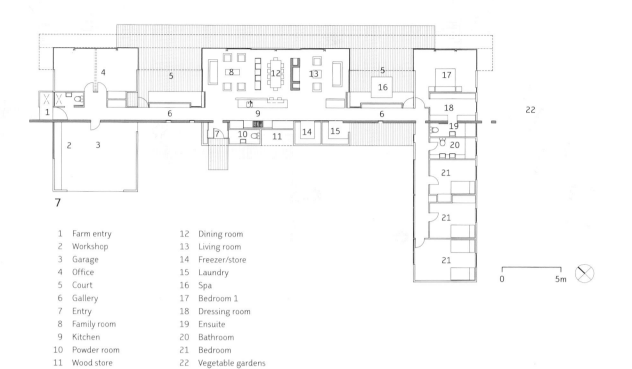

Photography: Patrick Reynolds and Joanna Aitken

1	Farm entry	12	Dining room
2	Workshop	13	Living room
3	Garage	14	Freezer/store
4	Office	15	Laundry
5	Court	16	Spa
6	Gallery	17	Bedroom 1
7	Entry	18	Dressing room
8	Family room	19	Ensuite
9	Kitchen	20	Bathroom
10	Powder room	21	Bedroom
11	Wood store	22	Vegetable gardens

8   9

PENCALENICK HOUSE

POLRUAN, CORNWALL, UNITED KINGDOM

SETH STEIN ARCHITECTS

Pencalenick House is a holiday home for its owner and his family on a site overlooking the picturesque Fowey estuary. The brief required that the building respond to the site's topography, aspect and environment in a sensitive yet thoroughly contemporary manner.

The architect's response was a curved plan that followed the site contours and embedded the house in the steeply sloping hillside. A turf roof continues the landscape while the perimeter indicates the structural form beneath; a line of glazing set at the same level as the grass denotes the internal circulation spine linking the various living spaces and the retaining wall against the hill. From the water the long volume is clearly book-ended into the hill by means of inserted Cornish slate retaining walls that also facilitate changes in level within the building and the landscape beyond.

The site is adjacent to national trust forest and is crossed by the historic Hall Walk so the project was sensitive from a planning point of view. The footprint of a demolished Victorian isolation hospital on the site was helpful as it left an established occupation area that created the parameters for locating the new structure.

The site was delineated via a new earth retaining concrete structure creating a shelf upon which to construct the glue-laminated timber frame structure of the house.

The green roof, seeded with a bespoke mixture of local grasses, is supported off the timber structure in a 900-millimetre-thick roof cassette that both insulates the building below and conceals its form when viewed from higher elevations. The range of natural finishing materials – cedar external cladding, Cornish slate, salvaged elm used for internal floors and joinery, sandblasted glass for the gallery bridge – emphasises the elemental nature of the setting and provides an interplay of texture and form throughout the course of the day. The overall effect is a building that, although uncompromisingly contemporary, sits very comfortably within the surrounding woodland.

Caradon Council awarded the house the Caradon Design Award for both the Best New Housing Design and Best Overall Scheme of 2007.

1   *The deployment of natural materials – cedar, elm and Cornish slate – in the building envelope allows the architecture to harmonise in its setting*

1

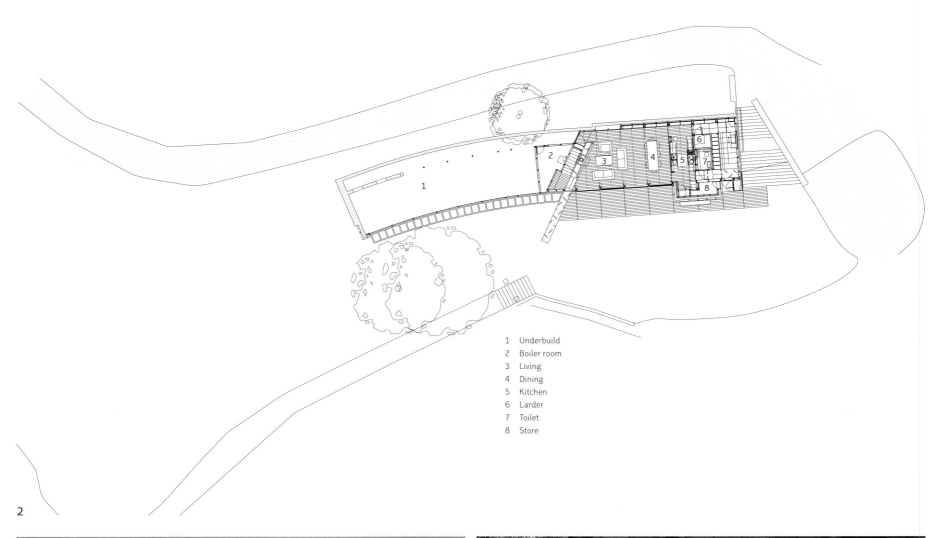

2

1 Underbuild
2 Boiler room
3 Living
4 Dining
5 Kitchen
6 Larder
7 Toilet
8 Store

3

4

2 Level 1 floor plan

3 The gentle curve of the plan is set out in sympathy with the existing site contours and allows the building to nestle into the landscape

4 The timber arrangement on the upper level of the south elevation provides solar shade and ventilation to the bedrooms and bathrooms

5 The double-height reception space on level 1 features a spacious dining area and log fire; floor-to-ceiling glazing on the south elevation offers views over the Fowey estuary

6 The double-height open-plan reception features a library wall and mezzanine level; books are an important element in the house and the area has a strong literary history, its most noted resident being Daphne du Maurier

7 Bedroom on level 2

8 Bathroom on level 2

Photography: Richard Davies

6

7

8

5

PENINSULA RESIDENCE

MORNINGTON PENINSULA, VICTORIA, AUSTRALIA

GREGORY BURGESS PTY LTD ARCHITECTS

Conceived as a weekend retreat for two extended families and their friends, this dwelling is discreetly hidden from the main-road traffic by a dense thicket of coastal casuarinas. On crossing this threshold the visitor emerges into a long, straight, treed avenue, which creates a formal edge to a more casual indigenous landscape and begins to frame distant views of Westernport Bay.

The drive peels off into a generous porte-cochère contained by an earth berm and grove of casuarinas to the west and the house to the east, which extends undulating rammed-earth walls and a low spreading canopy as a gesture of enclosure and welcome. The courtyards behind those walls are consequently protected from southwesterly squalls.

The house perches on the elevated edge of a gentle incline falling down to a sandy beach. It seems to be temporarily poised in its restless search for balance between convergence and divergence: the need for transparency, expansive views and wider connections and conversely the need for intimacy, refuge and enclosure. Externally this is expressed as a series of swirling roofs riding each other like waves, each one straining to see over the other, washing over an earth-wall base that flexes back on itself, anchoring against the tidal flux.

Inside, the plan fans, unfolding, bending and gathering its inner space before connecting with the outer foreground of grasses, the middle distance of coastal scrub and the long thin dissolving horizon of bay, island and sky. The interior has its own geology – a sense of being hollowed out of the living earth, cave-like, but with multiple interconnecting and overlapping chambers, each with its own particular purpose and dynamic aperture to land, sea and sky. Through a simultaneous experience of radial expansion with the wider environment and convergent focus of this same environment, it was hoped that the site and its multivariate forces might become palpable and meaningful to the dweller and so, over time, offer many small epiphanies of self, others and spirit of place.

1

1   View from southeast
2   View from northwest
3   Living room
4   View from entry to main stair looking through to living

2

4

3

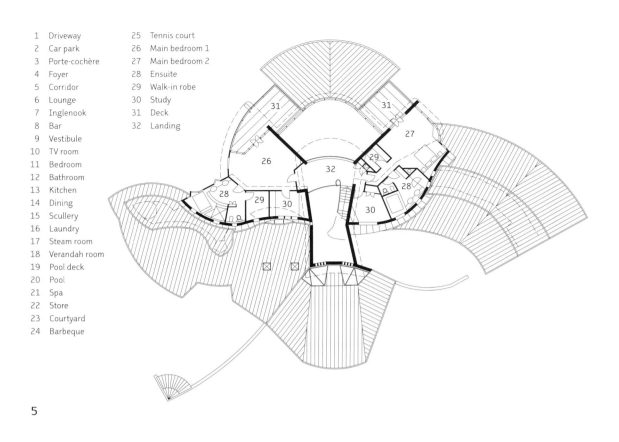

5

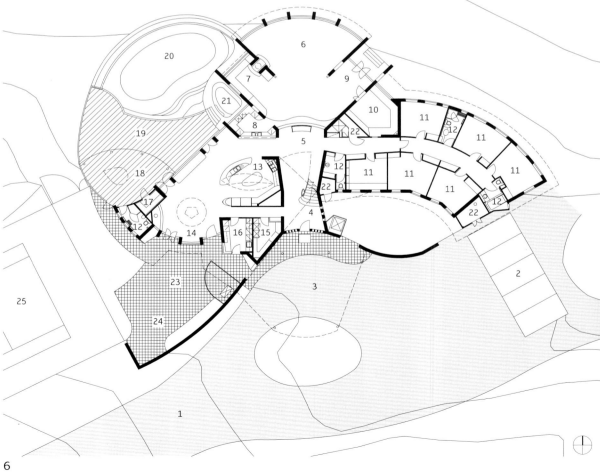

6

7

8

Photography: Derek Swalwell

PLUG-IN COTTAGE

IRELAND

MACGABHANN ARCHITECTS

Located on the banks of an estuary in northwest Ireland, the Plug-in Cottage consists of two extensions to an existing traditional cottage. The original cottage at the heart of this project is one room deep and three rooms long with a narrow linear form. This design sought to preserve the familiar form to maintain the architectural heritage and historical memory of the site while addressing the tectonic requirements of providing more accommodation for the family.

The original cottage dates from the early 1900s and, as with many other buildings of this type, fell into disrepair in the 1970s. It was restored and re-occupied in the 1990s and then subsequently extended in 2003-04. The original cottage was oriented with little regard for views or passive solar heat gain, evidence that such considerations were of little importance to the original habitants. To its current occupants, however, they are of the utmost importance. The site's far-reaching views of the sea and mountains are spectacular.

The design is pod/plug-in architecture meets the traditional Irish cottage. The design's overall form is a development of a diagrammatic plan that encompasses three key considerations: the sun's path, the various striking views and an intervention that has the least impact on the form of the original cottage. The occupants of the cottage chose to remain resident while the works were carried out and this programmatic requirement of the extension became part of the aesthetic. The brief included a large living room to take full advantage of the sun and the sweeping views, a new master bedroom and a laundry/utility room. The existing interior of the cottage was also subtly re-planned.

1   Living room
2   'Plug-ins'
3   Master bedroom and utility
4   Living room entrance

Photography: Ros Kavanagh

2

3

4

POND HOUSE

LONG ISLAND, NEW YORK, USA

LEROY STREET STUDIO

This house's site is a long narrow sloping strip of land that terminates at a saltwater pond. The project consists of three primary volumes as well as a pool house and detached garage and gym. The two private wings - one for parents and one for the children - are connected at the central public wing. The links between the volumes - the bridge, stairs and underground tunnel - blur the boundaries between the buildings. The children's wing acts as a gatehouse marking the pedestrian entry to the site. A path of stone planks leads up to shallow steps on an external walk carved through the first building and into a court, containing a grove of birch trees, defined by two buildings and a glass bridge overhead. From the glass front door it is possible to see the first view of the water through the living room.

The placement of the structures, each a modern interpretation of the vernacular form, creates a boundary that visually protects the more communal spaces within the other two wings. The more solid private wings provide shelter from the primarily glass public wing, which opens onto a public courtyard in the centre of the site. The buildings are clad in a white-painted cedar rain screen with cedar shingled roof - traditional materials that are detailed to create an abstract skin that is interrupted by large-scale aluminium curtain walls and windows. The interiors are rendered in shades of white with lacquered millwork and light oak floors creating a subtle and suffused background for structurally expressive stainless steel tie rods, cable-suspended stairs and floating bridges.

The simplicity of the structures accentuates and strengthens the impact of the interstitial spaces where volumes collide, creating a context for the sculptural stairways, bridges, catwalks, walkthroughs and terraces.

1

1 View from south reveals the home's relationship to pool, pergola and landscape

2 The east elevation faces Georgica Pond

2

3 Pool and pergola with view beyond of
   Georgica Pond

4,6 Two-storey living room: glassed wall allows
     views of the pond beyond

5 Floor plan

7 Daughter's bedroom

Photography: Adrian Wilson

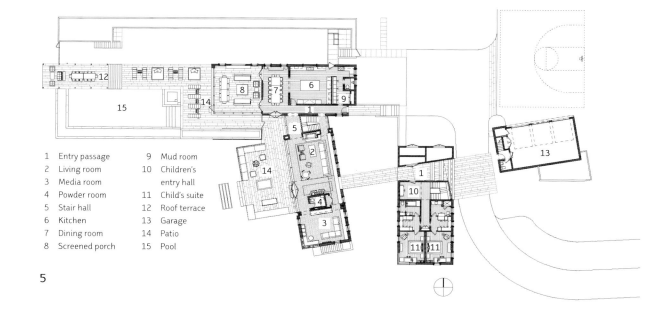

1 Entry passage   9   Mud room
2 Living room   10   Children's
3 Media room   entry hall
4 Powder room   11   Child's suite
5 Stair hall   12   Roof terrace
6 Kitchen   13   Garage
7 Dining room   14   Patio
8 Screened porch   15   Pool

5

6

4

7

POUND RIDGE HOUSE

POUND RIDGE, NEW YORK, USA

HARIRI & HARIRI – ARCHITECTURE

Inspired by Noguchi's stone sculptures and translucent 'Akari' lamps, this 420-square-metre home is sited on the highest elevation of a 2-hectare property with a tranquil, Zen-like setting. The architecture of this home interprets and internalises the landscape of tall trees and rock outcroppings, offering the properties of intangible time and light.

The house is composed of three interlocking volumes: the entry, living, and fitness/meditation volumes.

The entry volume is a vertical space two-and-a-half-storeys high. It takes the form of a vertical void and is the heart of the house. This void contains different levels and provides vertical and horizontal circulation to different parts of the house. It is enclosed by translucent fibreglass curtain walls, allowing soft light into the void while a series of windows with clear glass frame different parts of the landscape. The main element of this highly sculpted and articulated space is a staircase wrapping around a curved stucco wall, connecting different parts and levels of the house.

The living volume contains all the private spaces including bedrooms on the lower floor with the public spaces (living/dining) up above.

The fitness/meditation volume interlocks with the living and entry volume via the kitchen and family room on one level, and the gym on the lower level with the garage down below.

Capturing the very essence of nature through material, light and space, the Pound Ridge House evokes dynamic reactions and emotions in its occupants and visitors.

Opposite   Entry view

2   Exterior view from driveway

3   Living room with fireplace

4   Entry staircase

5   Floor plan

6   View from family room

7   Master bedroom

8   Dining room

9   Master bathroom

Photography: Harry Zernike

7

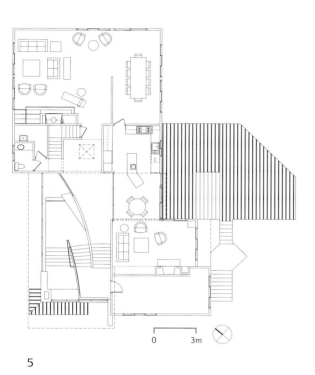

5

8

6

9

0   3m

PULL HOUSE

BRATTLEBORO, VERMONT, USA

PROCTER:RIHL

This house embraces the local architectural tradition while revisiting the barn prototype. A simple pitched-roof 'barn' has had one corner pulled out and moved diagonally from its rectangular loci. This has folded the entry gable façade from the ridge and created a strong diagonal south façade. These simple distortions are juxtaposed with the north side of the building, which appears quite ordinary. The folded gable of the west entry façade is painted with a strong colour to accent its difference. The east and north façades are clad with rough timber, which has been coloured to look like old weathered barn board, with random openings. The roof is clad with standing-seam metal, which is widely used locally.

Internally, the diagonal distortion generates a dramatic space resulting in the illusion of a larger living room. Windows are positioned judiciously to extend views out to the landscape.

The house is an energy-efficient super-insulated house with an air exchange ventilation system and triple-glazed windows. It has a 5-star energy rating with similarly rated appliances and 5–26 watt wired-in CFL lighting. Construction materials include structural insulated panels (SIPs) with 200-millimetre foam walls, a 300-millimetre foam sloped ceiling, and a trussed roof with 600 millimetres of blown-in cellulose. This compact plan four-bedroom, four-bathroom house is achieved within 210 square metres. Modest amounts of glazing are employed to reduce heat loss and heating is electric with future solar provision in radiant floor slabs.

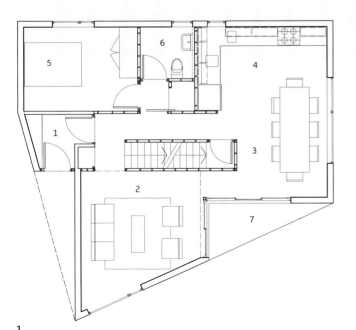

1

1   Entry
2   Living
3   Dining
4   Kitchen
5   Bedroom
6   Bathroom
7   Porch
8   Open living room
9   Loft/study
10 Master bedroom
11 Master bathroom

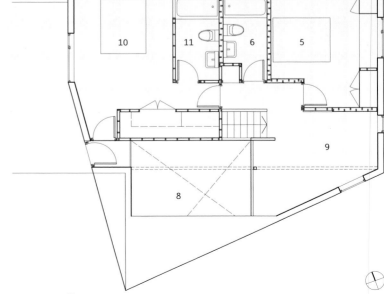

2

QUEENSTOWN RESIDENCE

QUEENSTOWN, NEW ZEALAND

RICE & SKINNER (IN CONJUNCTION WITH MURRAY COCKBURN PARTNERSHIP)

The brief for the Queenstown Residence was to provide the owner with an understated and warm holiday home. The 7235-square-metre site is located on the side of a mountain overlooking a river, with no other buildings in sight. So as not to disturb this landscape too greatly, the owner wanted the house to be as invisible as possible, while still taking advantage of one of the most beautiful sites that nature could offer.

The proposal was to literally bury the house. The 340-square-metre building has a linear plan, allowing it to run along the contour of the site and make the most of the stunning views. The site for the house was dug into the side of the mountain and when construction was completed the soil was reinstated on top of the house and planted with local grasses and shrubs.

Materials used in construction, the majority of which were sourced locally, were soft, simple and natural and the colours within the interior spaces are mostly intrinsic to these materials. A pool intersects the two primary zones of the house, while extensive terrace areas open out from the four bedrooms and the living and kitchen area.

1   Entry
2   Passage/library
3   Garage
4   Mud room/drying room
5   Laundry
6   Bathroom
7   Powder room
8   Living room
9   Kitchen/dining
10 Pantry
11 Cellar
12 Bedroom
13 Ensuite
14 Walk-in robe
15 Pool
16 Terrace
17 Plant room

1

0   5m

2

1 Floor plan
2 South elevation
3 Entry
4 View of pool
5 Living room

Photography: Suellen Boag and Martin Hill

3

4   5

RESIDENCE AMID THE INDIAN PAINTBRUSH

TETON COUNTY, WYOMING, USA

DUBBE-MOULDER ARCHITECTS

Utilising traditional log and stone materials, this home displays texture, site and functional space in a way that epitomises the idyllic mountain retreat. The goal of the design was to create an authentic Western lodge with respect for the original Rocky Mountain lodges scattered throughout the region. This retreat evokes the peace and serenity of its natural surroundings with accommodation for modern day technology and comfort. Particular attention was paid to the need for prominent outdoor living spaces designed for entertaining and relaxing with friends.

The structure is built into the side of a steep slope that virtually hugs the hillside. As a result, each of the three floors has grade-level access to an exterior living space or yard. This design puts each indoor and outdoor living space at an elevation that yields breathtaking views, both nearby and distant. To facilitate easy transitions from each floor, guests can either take the stairs or the elevator running from the first floor garage/games room/exercise room to the second-floor living room, kitchen and master bedroom and the third-floor office and guest suites.

The feeling of a Western lodge was created using a variety of regional materials on the exterior, such as a stone façade that frames reclaimed barn wood garage doors, floor-to-ceiling windows, exposed logs, hand-split cedar shingles and dry-stacked Montana stone. Exterior patios, terraces and decks work with these materials to create comfortable outdoor living spaces. The overall ambiance is further enhanced by a natural stone staircase, which gently climbs the grade to the main entrance of the home.

Upon entry, visitors are met with a spacious great room with log rafters, a rich hickory floor, plentiful windows and a massive stone fireplace that combined emanate a warm, golden glow. The room is designed to be a social hub with panoramic views of the Jackson Hole Valley.

Several unique outdoor living spaces are provided throughout the residence, including a sod roof over the garage, which reaches to a large deck wrapping the kitchen, dining and great room, creating the perfect venue for outdoor dinner parties or a quiet visit. Additional outdoor living spaces are the screened porch off the kitchen, which is an ideal place to enjoy an evening without wind and insects and a private screened porch in the master suite, showcasing views of the Grand Tetons and providing access to the outdoor hot tub.

1   A simple, gridded glass wall at the stairwell provides an
    interesting backdrop for the serene setting afforded by the
    sod roof over the garage

2   *Second floor plan*

3   *The sod roof over the garage allows for tremendous sweeping views of the Jackson Hole valley*

4   *Third floor plan*

5   *The living room and its outdoor deck provide nearby views of the forest, as well as panoramic views of the valley below*

6   *Designing the house for the steep site allows for the ability to walk out to grade on each floor*

7   *The kitchen was completed with knotty alder cabinets*

8   *The screened dining porch is a great place to play a board game in a 'camp' atmosphere*

9   *Master bedroom and private screened porch accessing outdoor hot tub*

Photography: Cameron Nielsen, The Seen

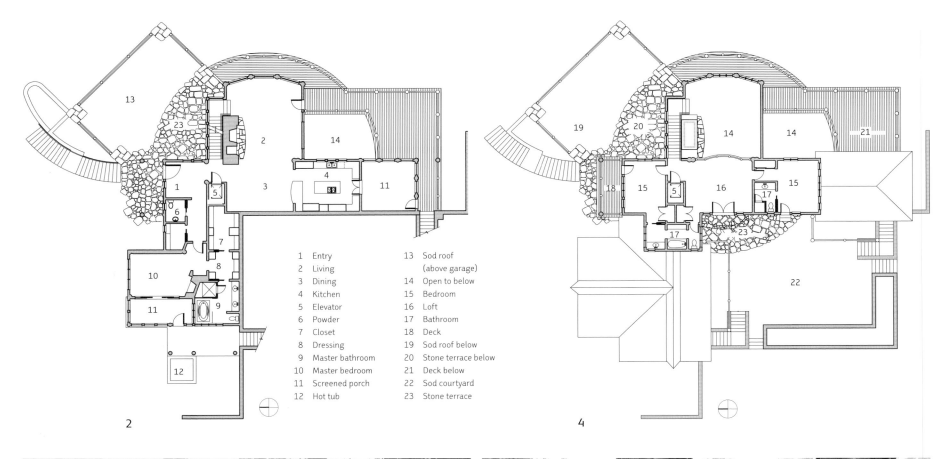

1	Entry	13	Sod roof
2	Living		(above garage)
3	Dining	14	Open to below
4	Kitchen	15	Bedroom
5	Elevator	16	Loft
6	Powder	17	Bathroom
7	Closet	18	Deck
8	Dressing	19	Sod roof below
9	Master bathroom	20	Stone terrace below
10	Master bedroom	21	Deck below
11	Screened porch	22	Sod courtyard
12	Hot tub	23	Stone terrace

2

4

3

5

6

7

8

9

RETREAT FOR A MOTHER AND DAUGHTER

LONG ISLAND, NEW YORK, USA

LEROY STREET STUDIO

A family weekend retreat with separate houses for a mother and her daughter was planned for a flat 5-hectare site, one block from the ocean in eastern Long Island. Leroy Street Studio developed a site response to tie the project's disparate elements together. To give the compound – divorced from its context by dense perimeter planting – a unique sense of place, the architects introduced dry-stack granite walls into the landscape, providing a secondary scale of internal and external spaces and a unifying texture.

House I

With its merging stone walls, the building's south entry façade appears solid and private, while its north side, facing the agricultural reserve, is expansively glazed.

The public wing is entered through a large entry cabinet that pierces the forecourt curtain wall. The entry hall opens onto interlocking ceiling-scapes: a lower dining room ceiling bleeds out into a covered porch and screened porch spaces, wrapping a soaring living room ceiling that flows down the main gallery axis and ends in the master bedroom. A two-storey stair hall is traversed by a glass bridge and top lit by a perimeter clerestory, making the roof float.

The gallery axis opens onto a sculpture court, ending in the master bedroom wing with a glazed bedroom sitting in its own private walled garden. Custom larch and aluminium cabinets wrap the kitchen, and a wall of pass-through cabinets separates the kitchen from a fully glazed breakfast room. Upstairs the glass bridge separates the guest bedroom, which opens onto its own sunset deck, from a ping-pong room and staff wing.

House II

This house is entered at its narrowest point through a glazed hall opening to a raised court of bamboo, extending up through an opening in the long, low roof plane. This roof continues into the public wing, opening again over the dining area to expose an upper, perpendicular roof floating out over the living room and outdoor porch. A long stone wall follows the upper roof plane out into the landscape, broken occasionally for cabinetry insertions, and ending in a reflecting pool, washing up against the outdoor porch. In contrast, the public wing is defined as a taut box of marching oak glulam portal frames wrapped in a continuous skin of louvres.

1   *View from northeast of both houses (daughter's at left and mother's at right)*
2   *Pavers form a footpath to daughter's house; view of mother's house beyond reflecting pool*
3   *Kitchen in mother's house leads into living room*
4   *Daughter's house master bedroom and adjoining covered patio maximise views of the preserve with floor-to-ceiling glass*

Photography: Paul Warchol

1

2

3

4

RIDGE HOUSE

SALT SPRING ISLAND, BRITISH COLUMBIA, CANADA

HELLIWELL + SMITH – BLUE SKY ARCHITECTURE

The Ridge House is the culmination of its owners' retirement dreams. They had owned the steep, heavily treed, hillside site for many years and carefully formulated their ideas for onsite development. They identified a narrow rocky ridge, running approximately east-west though a grove of small twisted arbutus, as the preferred building site.

Balanced on the spine of this rocky ridge, the linear house plan threads through the grove of arbutus opening to the light and views to the west - with the section determined by the topography. The rooms are all accessed off the central hallway, which the roof ridge is centered on. Moving through the house, the exposed rafters gradually invert into a butterfly roof opening to bring light into the main social areas. The hall expands in width as it moves towards the views.

Rainwater is channelled from the roof into an exaggerated scupper, which in turn funnels the water into a pond floating on the terrace roof. This pond is centred on the hall axis through the house and when full of water it acts as a small reflecting pond in celebration of plentiful rainfall.

This house builds upon the West Coast modern tradition of extending the interior living environments into site-specific landscapes. Its structure is clearly expressed with a Douglas fir post-and-beam system. The door and window systems are integral to the timber frame structure. Great attention has been paid to details and craftsmanship, resulting in a beautiful home balanced sensitively on its rocky forest ridge.

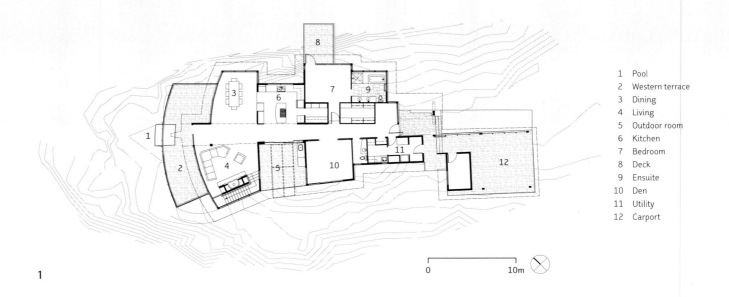

1   Pool
2   Western terrace
3   Dining
4   Living
5   Outdoor room
6   Kitchen
7   Bedroom
8   Deck
9   Ensuite
10 Den
11 Utility
12 Carport

1

0   10m

2

3

4

5

1   Main floor plan
2   West elevation
3   Exterior from northwest
4   Living room
5   Dining area

Photography: Gillean Proctor

RILEY HOUSE II

CONNECTICUT SHORELINE, USA

CENTERBROOK ARCHITECTS AND PLANNERS

Renovations and additions transformed an ordinary house, built in 1969, into an eccentric home recalling small love affairs with places around the world. At the front of the house, a new garage and garden shed addition join the original, but altered, gambrel roof house to evoke memories of the Cotswolds. At the rear, the pale-yellow stucco walls of the family and living room additions and a walled garden enclose an outdoor terrace, recalling the intimate courtyards and easy outdoor living of Provence and Umbria. Custom copper gutters, supported on overhanging cedar eave brackets, and copper leaders that spill their rainwater onto stones set on the terrace recall the simple elegance of the gardens of Kyoto.

Inside, the living room evokes a variety of images. Its ochre-stained concrete floor takes on the ruddy colours of the ancient Nabataean city of Petra, Jordan. The stucco fireplace, accented with stone inserts and flanked by colourfully tiled, miniature, house-like niches, captures the Spanish Colonial character of the American Southwest. Horizontally striped columns recollect the flourishes of Siena, Italy, and are capped with wooden salad bowls from Sierra Leone, Africa. Finally, an octagonal peristyle, supported by the striped columns, aspires to the Byzantine spatial delights of San Vitale in Ravenna, Italy. To add to the sense of threshold as one enters the columned living room, the floor steps down and the ceiling within the peristyle rises. Here is the centre of the owners' own universe, a sacred place.

The long dining room, accentuated by its 5-metre-long table, has the pretensions of the medieval halls of chateaux in the Loire Valley. The room is framed at the ceiling by rows of mahogany brackets carved in floral motif and supporting a series of wooden beams. The brackets impart a sense of life to the inanimate beams that is at the heart of the Renaissance buildings of Rome and Florence. Indeed, the stairway to the second floor takes its cues from Michelangelo's Laurentian Library in Florence.

Upstairs, the renovated master bedroom expands into an octagonal work studio. It is the vertical extension of the octagonal peristyle below and commands a panoramic view of the surrounding woods and gardens.

1   To the south, a garden and the stucco walls of the additions enclose an outdoor terrace
2   First floor plan
3   The octagonal peristyle in the living room
4   Outdoor terrace

Photography: Peter Aaron / Esto

1

3

1 Entry hall
2 Dining
3 Kitchen
4 Existing den
5 Family room
6 Living room
7 Music room
8 Boiler
9 Exercise room
10 Woodshop
11 Mud room
12 Wood shed
13 Potting shed
14 Bike shed
15 Garage
16 Fire wood
17 West terrace
18 South terrace
19 Garden

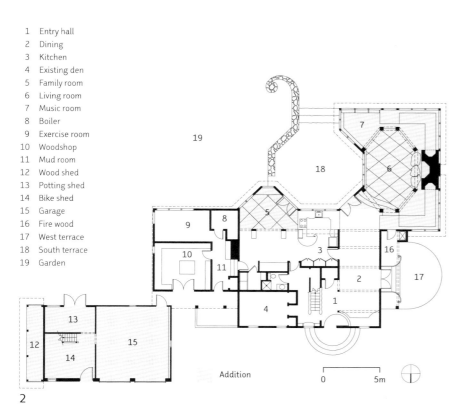

Addition

0   5m

2

4

ROBSON FARMHOUSE AT THE ROSSHILL VINEYARD

ORANGE, NEW SOUTH WALES, AUSTRALIA

KEITH PIKE ASSOCIATES

Rosshill is a boutique vineyard on 63 hectares just outside the town of Orange in New South Wales. The brief was for a large, low-maintenance house designed to look over the vineyard and take advantage of views over the property and of other important local features. A large wine cellar (to hold 40,000 bottles) with forklift access was also required.

The owners' extended family of children and grandchildren meant the house needed to accommodate large-scale entertaining and visitors staying over.

The house is sited on the side of a hill with the cellar partially buried underneath. Rainwater tanks are incorporated as architectural features. The bedroom accommodation is split, with the owners located in their own wing for privacy.

A large external north-facing terrace cantilevers east towards the vineyard and views across the dams. A 30-metre verandah fronts the entire main house, opening towards the view, and continues south, cantilevering out through an angled blade wall to take in a view of Mount Canobolis, the district's highest topographical feature.

A limited material palette of rendered masonry walls and extensive use of simple but articulated steelwork in the verandahs, balustrades and roof edges is used to impart the house with a robust yet serene presence in the landscape.

1   Overall view from northeast
2   The house nestles into the hillside
3   North deck with fireplace
4   Elevated verandah

1

4

2

3

5

6

7

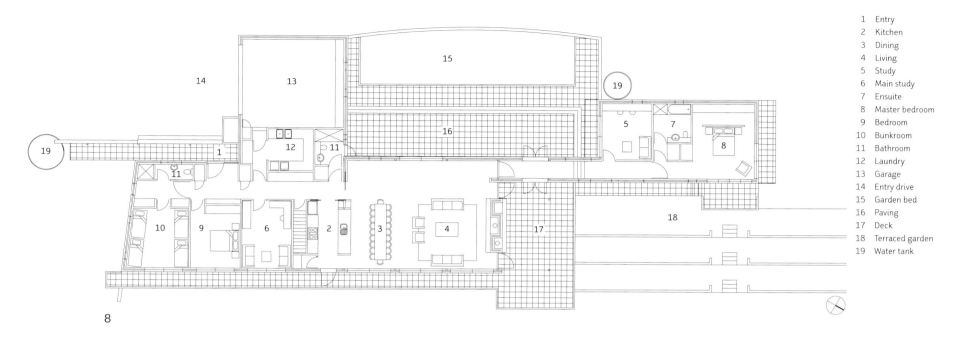

1	Entry
2	Kitchen
3	Dining
4	Living
5	Study
6	Main study
7	Ensuite
8	Master bedroom
9	Bedroom
10	Bunkroom
11	Bathroom
12	Laundry
13	Garage
14	Entry drive
15	Garden bed
16	Paving
17	Deck
18	Terraced garden
19	Water tank

8

9

10

5   *North deck with view across vineyard*

6   *View to master bedroom pavilion*

7   *View through house from courtyard garden*

8   *Floor plan*

9   *Living and dining room*

10 *Dining room looking to kitchen*

Photography: Colin Begg (1); Keith Pike (2,3,4,6,7); Adrian Boddy (5,9,10)

RURAL RETREAT ARCADIA

NEW SOUTH WALES, AUSTRALIA

ELEVEN ELEVEN DESIGN + DEVELOP

The key to this design lies in an awareness of the environment, containment of space and expression of form, rhythm and layering. To blend the home with the surrounding bushland, internal spaces admit and include the external. These spaces are defined by wall surfaces that open to vistas through light wells onto exterior surfaces and the surrounding bushland, framing views of horses in the fields. With the most spectacular of the property's views lying to the south, it was a challenge to orient the property towards this aspect while maintaining solar access. By working with the existing form and removing a dividing wall, the main living area now flows from north to south. The result is a complete transformation from the simple brick style of the original structure.

Environmental factors play an integral role in the home. Excavated water tanks, solar panels, heat deflection, cross ventilation and energy-efficient lighting are all utilised to maximise efficiency and comfort. The exterior stone has an earthy quality that firmly roots the building in the landscape. Visible from all rooms, it underpins the rustic feel of the house. The open-plan building, while inviting the outside in, has a comfortable private feeling created by the layout of the bedroom wings, which surround all the living spaces and frame the best views. By bringing the pastoral peacefulness of its surroundings into the house, a sense of tranquillity and escape is developed.

The client's willingness to take risks resulted in a warm, earthy living space delivered through textures, forms and an unconventional mix of materials. The use of steel and stone throughout the space continues the sense of being in the 'outback'. And, as with their natural counterparts, these surfaces will gain charm and beauty as their patinas develop through wear. The luxurious finishes to the interior and overall attention to detail - in particular the island bench, bar and the steel benchtop - are a triumph, and testimony to the combination of highly skilled tradespeople involved in the project. In this home, as in the natural environment, balance is fundamental; no singular aspect dominates, each exists in harmony with the other. The result is a space at once serviceable, comfortable and comforting.

1   This contemporary home features stone cladding with strong timber elements anchoring the structure within the rural landscape

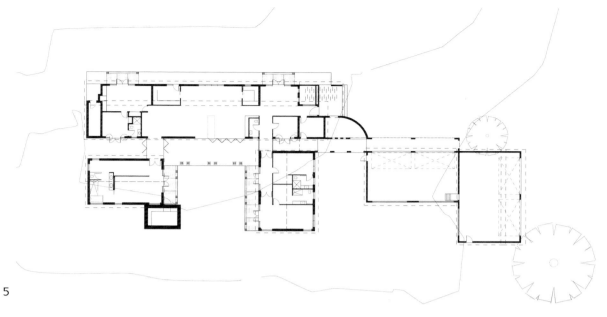

2 The stable complex was built in conjunction with the main house and reflects it in both architectural style and choice of materials

3 External view of entertaining and BBQ area rolling out onto the grassed courtyard

4 Stringybark timbers were used for this pergola, providing shade for bedrooms and framing views to the south

5 Floor plan

6 The central fireplace becomes the dividing element between the living and the dining spaces

7 Custom-designed 6-millimetre-thick floating steel shelving with polished concrete elements provides the link between rustic and modern

Photography: Eliot Cohen (1,3); Juliann Lupino (2,4,6,7)

5

6

7

SABER HOUSE

EAST HAMPTON, NEW YORK, USA

ALFREDO DE VIDO

Fifteen years ago, Alfredo De Vido designed this vacation house on eastern Long Island. When the owners relocated abroad, the house was sold to a couple with young children who wanted to change the spaces to reflect their own family lifestyle. They decided to engage the original architect to renovate the house and design a 230-square-metre addition.

In the resulting redesign, the owners' goals were achieved by means of two separate additions, one at the west end of the house and the other at the east end.

To make space for the addition on the west side of the house, a garage was removed and a large kitchen/dining/living area was added. This space became the focus of the house and offers easy access to the outdoor areas surrounding the swimming pool. Here, trellises define the outdoor spaces and walkways. The swimming pool fences are required for safety reasons and come with the added bonus of keeping out predatory animals.

The eastern addition is a two-storey structure that includes a garage and, on the second floor, a TV and games room. The bright colour schemes that were an integral part of the original house have been continued throughout the two additions.

1

2

3

4

1 Blue colour scheme of the entranceway complements the dark colour of the original house

2 The original house was sited among magnificent white pines; the addition is carefully fitted into the landscape

3 Lighting designed by the architect complements architecture

4 The kitchen is designed with ample space for several people to join in meal preparation

5 View of new living space

Photography: Todd Mason (1,2,3); Paul Warchol (4,5)

5

THE SAGAPONAC HOUSE

LONG ISLAND, NEW YORK, USA

HARIRI & HARIRI – ARCHITECTURE

This 430-square-metre house is located on a hectare of wooded land in the middle of the former potato fields between the fashionable South and East Hampton areas of Long Island, New York. Its spatial configuration invites a variety of personalities and occupants – from reclusive individuals to sociable couples or groups – to be 'original' and invent their own mode of habitation in this structure.

In contrast to most oversized showplaces, suburban mansions, and overstated country houses, this house is composed of two simple rectangular volumes forming an L-shaped plan. It frames and engages the landscape and the pleasures of being in the country. The centre of the house is the main public space, with a swimming pool, multilevel terraces and a covered porch with a shower. This space is accessible and visible from all other parts of the house, and at times it is visible to the neighbours and the street, becoming a stage for action and display. This private pool area is similar to some beaches in the area, which become stages for exhibitionism and spectatorship of parading bodies.

Inspired by Alberto Giacometti's sculpture *Figure in a Box Between Two Boxes Which Are Houses*, the Sagaponac House takes the form of a minimalist structure placed on a platform within an untouched natural landscape.

A large opening within each rectangular volume frames the private life within the house and in and around the pool beyond. These openings appear and disappear via a system of metal shutters mounted on the exterior walls, investigating the cultural definition of the domestic enclosure. These metal shutters not only act as a shield against intruders when no one is at home, they also reveal and conceal private and public hidden motivations, social interactions and exchanges within and beyond the house.

1

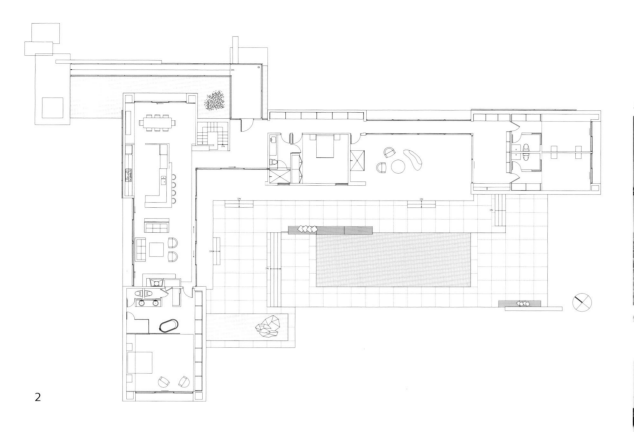

2

4

5

3

1 Entry view from driveway
2 Floor plan
3 View from garden with pool and pool deck
4 Kitchen and living room
5 Master bedroom

Photography: © Paul Warchol

SAPPHIRE RIDGE

WHITFORD, NEW ZEALAND

SOLUTIONS ARCHITECTURE LIMITED

This home occupies a small rural block in Whitford – ten minutes by car from the bustling town of Botany, near Auckland. Its position on the high point of the peninsula affords outstanding 360-degree views, with a northern aspect over Tamaki Strait, Waiheke Island and the Hauraki Gulf. The solar-heated swimming pool and tennis court are constructed on layers below the house to maintain view lines; they are also positioned symmetrically on the central axis of the dwelling.

The owners wanted a symmetrical look for the house, which contains three primary zones. One is a parents' wing complete with family room, kitchen, dining room, two bedrooms for grandchildren, library, office, craft room, master suite and lounge. The second is their son's wing, which incorporates two bedrooms, two bathrooms, a study/den, a master suite, dining and lounge. The third area is for entertaining and contains a great room with bar, an art gallery, a formal dining area with a 22-seat table, the home theatre, a caterer's kitchen, a cellar and two guest suites.

Plastered brick was used for its durability and aesthetics. A Gerard Senator shingle roof was chosen for its appearance and weatherproofing, an important factor considering the exposed nature of the site. The house also features the 'Control4' home automation system for lighting, comfort, audio and visual aspects with a fully integrated, under-floor heating system on the ground floor.

The infinity-edge pool tops off the understated and elegant outdoor areas. With solar-powered heating from the panels, the water is always temperate. The weir's black granite tiles help to maintain the warmth.

1   *Three entrances and garages from the south*
2   *Looking west across pool to conservatory and west loggia on ground floor, and great room and master suite deck on first floor*
3   *West view across first-floor decks, Whitford Creek in background*

1

3

2

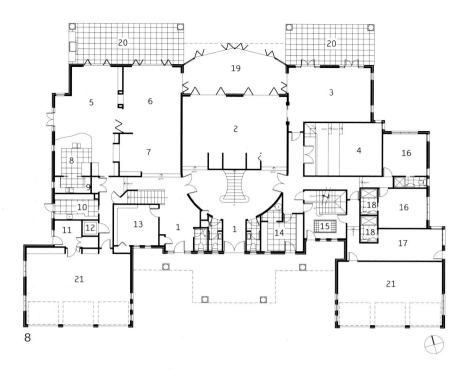

1 Foyer
2 Great room
3 Formal dining 1
4 Theatre
5 Family
6 Lounge
7 Formal dining 2
8 Kitchen
9 Scullery
10 Laundry
11 Workshop
12 Lift
13 Office
14 Caterers
15 Foyer
16 Guest bedroom
17 Gym
18 Ensuite
19 Conservatory
20 Loggia
21 Triple garage

8

9

10

4   Formal lounge in west wing

5   Entry and staircase to great room

6   Lounge in east wing

7   Master bedroom in east wing

8   Ground floor plan

9   Kitchen in west wing

10 Ensuite in west wing

Photography: Kallan MacLeod

SELF-SUFFICIENT HOUSE

KANGAROO VALLEY, NEW SOUTH WALES, AUSTRALIA

UTZ-SANBY ARCHITECTS

The brief was to build a weekend retreat – a simple house that would respond to the local climate, the immediate site and the surrounding landscape. The 65-hectare site is surrounded by steep sandstone escarpments to the south and views down the valley to the north. There were no existing services on the site.

The house is naturally protected from the cold southerly winds by the slope of the land, and is open to the north to maximise views and sun. The experience inside the house is predominantly a feeling of being connected to the landscape, sky and surrounding escarpments. While very comfortable, the house, at 140 square metres, is extremely compact and has been stripped of any superfluous elements to the basic functions of everyday living as a means of controlling both cost and energy consumption.

The extruded rectangular form of the house stretches along the contours of the site and enables a view from every room, reminiscent of a railway carriage. The circulation spine is aligned with and frames views of the two wooded 'fingers', enclosing the site to the east and west. The continuous roof and ceiling plane can be read from both inside and outside the building and is probably the most important element of the design, as it not only provides shelter and unity, but is pitched precisely to exclude summer sun, invite winter sun and to ensure maximum water collection.

The decision to make the house entirely self-sufficient was made early in the project as a means of controlling the budget. This then drove the design process towards a well-considered environmental response in terms of form, structure and materials and led the practice to explore new sustainable systems and technologies.

Opposite   The southern side of the house is more solid and protected from cold winds by the natural contours of the site

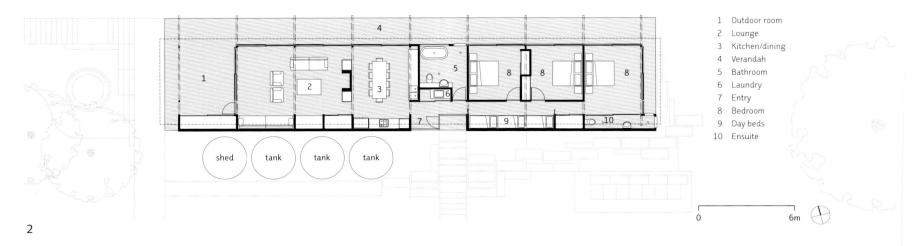

1   Outdoor room
2   Lounge
3   Kitchen/dining
4   Verandah
5   Bathroom
6   Laundry
7   Entry
8   Bedroom
9   Day beds
10   Ensuite

0   6m

2

3

4

2 Floor plan

3 A circular concrete fire-pit uses a corrugated steel sheet as formwork and blends in with the house and water tanks

4 The living room has a mono-pitched roof

5 The clients wanted to emulate the feel of a traditional 'eat-in' country kitchen

6 The master bedroom is open on two sides

7 The main bathroom has a flip-up panel to enhance the bathing experience

Photography: Ben Wrigley - Photohub (1,4,5,6,7); Jamie Cobeldick, courtesy of Trends Publishing International (3)

5

6

7

SHALKAI

SALT SPRING ISLAND, BRITISH COLUMBIA, CANADA

HELLIWELL + SMITH – BLUE SKY ARCHITECTURE

Situated in a peaceful south-facing oak meadow high above the Gulf Islands, Shalkai is designed as a retreat and meditation environment for its owners. The clients fell in love with the site and wanted to retain its natural state. The architects and builders took great care to preserve the landscape throughout the building process. The house was designed to curve around a grove of Garry oaks while following the existing contours of the sloping hillside. A lower landscape roof covering the central hallway of the house ties the building to the hillside. A rising and undulating roof opens the building to the views and south light on the site.

The house plan is like a path on a level contour across the hillside, moving dynamically from social rooms to private ones. Spaces are discovered in glimpses as the hallway continually wraps around the hill. The roof structure is exposed with solid fir rafters and decking dynamically balanced on fir posts, which in turn are balanced on horizontal beams and vertical columns. The rafters rise and fall to create the gentle undulating form of the roof covering all of the major spaces. The den, meditation room and gallery/hallway are under the lower green roof. The split between the two roofs allows for clerestory windows into the great room that both balance light and provide opportunities for cross ventilation. Large overhangs shelter the house from the southern sun.

A covered outdoor room provides all-season outdoor living while creating a split in the plan between social and private spaces. The entrance, guest area, office area, great room and kitchen are linked to the main bedroom suite by a transparent hallway that is positioned around the oak grove and the outdoor room.

The window system is integral with the timber frame structure. The structural frame gives visual strength and warmth to the house and the siding and the doors throughout the house are finely detailed with a cedar and copper inlay. The final result is a beautiful home that sits naturally in its glorious setting.

1   Entry garden
2   View from covered terrace
3   Covered terrace
4   Gallery hallway at bedroom

1

3

4

2

5

6

7

1 Library
2 Bathroom A
3 Bathroom B
4 Gallery
5 Bedroom
6 Covered terrace
7 Living room
8 Dining room
9 Kitchen
10 Guest bedroom
11 Entry terrace
12 Utility
13 Bathroom C
14 Office
15 Oak grove

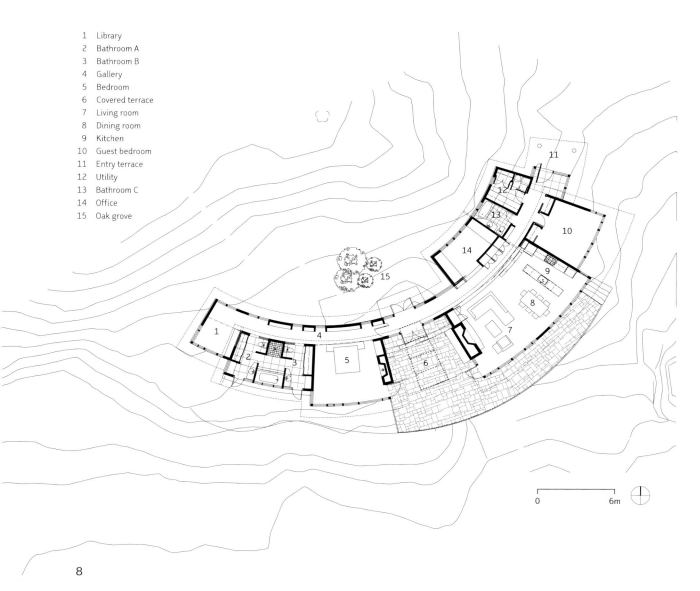

0   6m

5   Main living spaces
6   Ensuite
7   Kitchen
8   Floor plan
9   Bedroom
10 South terrace

Photography: Gillean Proctor and Peter Powles

8

9

10

SHIFT COTTAGE

GEORGIAN BAY, ONTARIO, CANADA

SUPERKÜL INC | ARCHITECT

The site for this 185-square-metre family cottage, on the edge of a 4-hectare Precambrian granite island, was chosen for its topography and orientation. Nestled into the rock and against a line of trees, the cottage is positioned to take full advantage of the site's natural beauty and protection from the often-extreme weather.

A glass walkway links the cottage's two volumes. The living spaces, including a screened-in porch at the north end, are closest to the shore; bedrooms are located further inland, against a line of trees. Wrapped in knotty cedar board and deck, the textured modernist vocabulary of the exterior is continued on the interior, where cedar and painted pine board, glulam beams and cedar deck are the primary finishes, composed to create an elegant and warm home away from home.

Window openings are aligned throughout to allow cross ventilation and views through the cottage from the treeline to the open water in front. A cedar deck around the cottage folds down to meet the rock; it hosts outdoor living spaces including a contained children's play area and a private outdoor shower.

In keeping with the family's intergenerational stewardship of the island, the cottage was designed to tread lightly on the land. Materials and equipment were delivered by barge. This delivery method restricted both the weight and size of what could be shipped, and the design evolved quickly to use only materials and tools that could be moved and managed without the use of heavy equipment. The resulting design used locally sourced lightweight structural and building materials, much of it available in smaller components that could be managed and moved by one pair of hands.

As the cottage is sited in a natural clearing, no trees were removed. Pier foundations obviated any blasting of the rock and allow for undercroft cooling. The cottage is passively illuminated, ventilated and cooled, and the use of local and natural materials left largely in their unfinished states will leave a smaller footprint.

1   A cedar deck on three sides folds down to meet the
    granite island

2   A dry-laid stone fireplace faces both the living room and
    the screened porch

3   A view from the master bedroom across the deck to the
    dining room

4   View through the glass link to a small reading desk and
    the trees beyond

5   Floor plan

Photography: Tom Arban Photography Inc.

1

1 Screened porch
2 Living
3 Kitchen
4 Dining
5 Deck
6 Glass link
7 Storage with loft
  sleeping above
8 Study
9 Bedroom
10 Master bedroom
11 Outdoor shower

SIMPSON HOUSE

ATHERTON TABLELANDS, QUEENSLAND, AUSTRALIA

DAVID LANGSTON-JONES

The Simpson House sits on the brow of a field among pastureland and is positioned to act as a foil to the existing farm sheds and water tanks. Its diagonal placement visually detaches the new pavilion from the adjacent outhouses, creates a sheltered courtyard and opens up the living space to the pastoral panorama on two sides. To meet the rigorous demands of an extremely limited budget the planning and construction of the house employed tight planning and pre-fabrication strategies to limit the amount and duration of construction. Therefore, in spite of the available land, the size and form of the house were determined to a large degree by what was affordable.

The 9- by 9-metre square plan with mezzanine deck over the living area provides maximum internal volume and planning freedom for minimum wall and floor coverage. This also creates the deepest plan, and thereby maximum shade, for a given number of roof sheets, which is an important consideration in the climatic context of the tropical far north of Australia. To facilitate construction, as many building elements as possible were standardised and pre-fabricated, including the steel structure with standard staircase details, steel infill wall framing, glazing and joinery. An all-weather plywood floor that could be put down quickly provided a construction platform, after which it was left exposed, sanded and sealed. As a result the construction period was precisely 12 weeks, minimising the builders' exposure to the harsh Far North Queensland sun.

It is no coincidence that an apparent visual similarity with the traditional Queenslander house typology exists. The design of this house is a response from first principles to the ongoing climatic and economic challenges that have always characterised Queensland's domestic architecture.

1

2

1 The new pavilion sits on the diagonal to act as a foil to the existing sheds
2 The glazed bay of the living room projects into the landscape towards the pastoral prospect
3 The central structural tower forms a series of intimate spaces around it
4 Floor plan
5 Night view

Photography: Aaron Leong

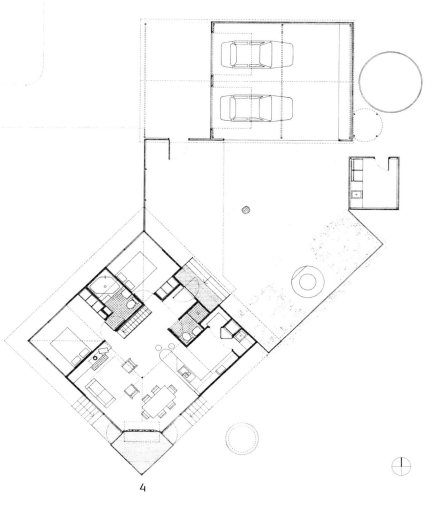

4

3

5

SLOUGH POND RESIDENCE

TURO, CAPE COD, MASSACHUSETTS, USA

HAMMER ARCHITECTS

The Outer Cape, including the towns of Wellfleet and Truro, was largely undeveloped prior to the Second World War. In the years following the war, many visitors discovered the beauty of this end of Cape Cod with its unspoiled ocean beaches and freshwater ponds. The region began to attract a community of artists, writers, playwrights, educators and architects. A number of modern houses were designed in a manner influenced by the International Style yet uniquely adapted to the local landscape and regional vernacular. Notable among the architects who built houses for themselves and their clients are Marcel Breuer, Serge Chemayeff and Walter Gropius. The houses nestled lightly into the landscape and were informed by the modern precept of visually connecting interior and exterior spaces.

Henry Hebbeln was a modern architect with offices in New York City. He studied with Eero Saarinen at Cranbrook Academy in Michigan and designed many residences strongly influenced by the International Style. This mid-century modern house in the Wellfleet Woods is his only known building on Cape Cod. The original portion of the house was constructed as a barracks during the Second World War. The Hebbeln-designed five-bay butterfly roof addition was constructed in 1953. The architecture is notable for its large expanses of glass, built-in furniture, wood beam structure and tongue-and-groove siding.

The house is located within the Cape Cod National Seashore Park and is sited on a knoll overlooking two kettle ponds. The 2008 addition by Hammer Architects includes a master bedroom suite, study and kitchen on the first floor. A new roof deck overlooking the ponds is accessed through the second-floor home office. The renovated portion of the residence houses the living/dining room and two guest bedrooms.

The design challenge was to integrate a 21st-century fully insulated and code-compliant year-round addition with a mid-20th-century modern 'summer cottage'. New windows are carefully designed to relate to the fenestration pattern of the existing wing and provide natural ventilation and views. The materials were selected to age appropriately and blend into the context. The sunscreen, in addition to shading the windows and providing a covered outdoor dining terrace, knits the entire complex together as a unified composition.

1

Photography: Bill Lyons

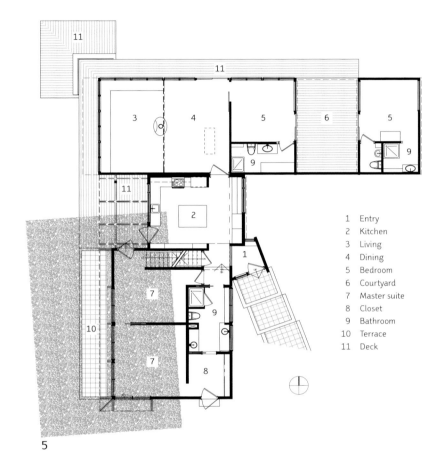

1   Entry
2   Kitchen
3   Living
4   Dining
5   Bedroom
6   Courtyard
7   Master suite
8   Closet
9   Bathroom
10 Terrace
11 Deck

5

2

3

4

STONE HOUSE

MORNINGTON PENINSULA, VICTORIA, AUSTRALIA

GREGORY BURGESS PTY LTD ARCHITECTS

Out of sight from the main road behind orchards and extensive landscaping, this house nestles in a long shallow valley forming a natural cliff-top amphitheatre above Westernport Bay. The entry off the curving driveway/courtyard pushes down through massive stone screen walls into a double-height space lit by an arching clerestory. Stairs lead down to the living areas and the views beyond, and up to the bedrooms and studies. A palette of complementary materials is used throughout: the timber's qualities are highlighted by being brought together with stone and copper in dramatically modulated natural light. The rough-textured stonework contrasts with the delicate detailing of the timber ceilings and balustrades, and throughout a sense of intimate enclosure is set against visual connections to the gardens, grasslands and seascape beyond.

In its demanding maritime location, the building has a robust and hardy appearance at the arrival point: a constructed landscape of sweeping stone and sand. However the jagged two-storey stone walls are softened by a series of cascading canopies with warm timber linings that shelter a welcoming path to the entry door. Inside, a timber floor flows between stone walls, leading through to the family living rooms that overlook the ocean. The Sydney blue gum staircase, cascading around a massive stone bastion like a waterfall, gives access to the bedrooms upstairs, and its movement is emphasised by the design of the balustrade, which combines timber with delicately curved copper rods. Above this double-height space the arched ceiling is pierced by clerestory windows, and its gentle curve is emphasised by light timber battens fixed across the surface. The combination of these three-dimensional arcs gives life and interest to the entry space, providing ever-changing relationships between the different elements and combinations of material and shape.

From the entry the external stone walls step down towards the coast, forming a solid base to the house above while a more delicate series of structures enclose the living spaces. Vertical timber batten and board cladding of radially sawn silvertop ash has copper details, and the attached conservatory is formed from robust recycled karri timbers with louvred glazing. To one side a timber deck extends out and, folding up and around, creates a swimming pool platform and spa area with extensive use of jarrah. A series of protected terraces and balconies provide spectacular views across Westernport Bay towards the islands.

1   View from east
2   View across pool from north
3   Porte-cochère from west

1

3

2

4

5

4   Ceiling over entry
5   Living room looking towards kitchen and dining
6   First floor plan
7   Ground floor plan
8   Kitchen looking through to conservatory
9   Bathroom

Photography: John Gollings

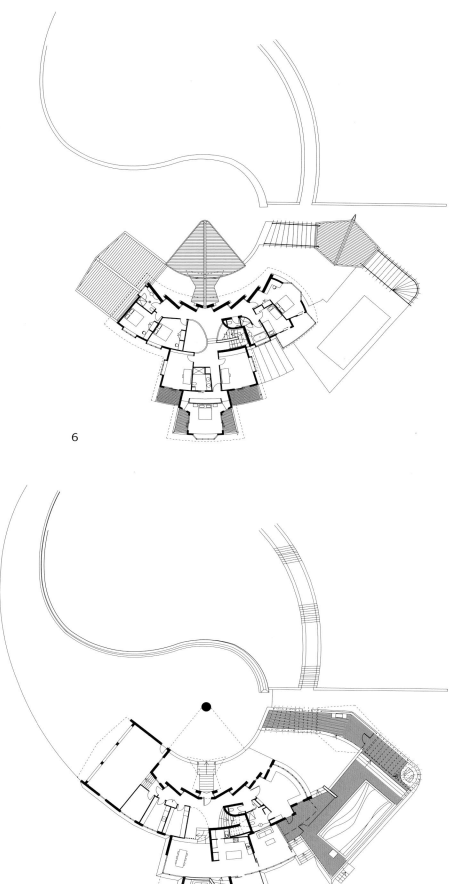

0   10m

SUNSHINE CANYON HOUSE

BOULDER, COLORADO, USA

JONATHAN SCHLOSS / ARCHITECT

This house occupies a hillside in Sunshine Canyon outside Boulder, Colorado. While the site has spectacular views and a lush, isolated setting, the constrained original house lacked a sense of interior movement and strong connection to its surroundings. The project objective was to address these shortcomings, substantially expand and gut-renovate the entire house and ultimately create a new residence with generous living spaces and a definite sense of place.

The core of the house is a collection of horizontal volumes and planes of white stucco and wood. At the edges of this white core, Brazilian redwood structures ease the transition to nature. A combination of extended redwood decks, balconies, towers and glass volumes occupy the perimeter. These intersecting geometries allow for vertical movement and unobstructed horizontal views while giving the exterior a rhythm of form and material that contributes a human scale to the house. The horizontal wood screens and siding add texture and accentuate the home's horizontality in the mountain landscape.

A new stair tower designed for the eastern façade allows an open and natural transition between the common areas of both floors and forms a strong connection with the entry - from the front to the back of the house. The redwood-clad stair tower also adds depth to what was an otherwise flat façade and separates public and private spaces.

Several portions of the house have been opened up and expanded, refocused and reconfigured. For example, the redwood screen and glass volume that is now the entry extends the previously undefined entryway, while planar elements such as the flat roofs and clerestory are reintroduced to present a more transparent and permeable façade.

Glass volumes and finishes blur the boundary between indoor and outdoor spaces, particularly in the master bathroom, where one may bathe while seemingly immersed in the front grove of trees, and in the living room, where expansive interior spaces help unite unobstructed views to the landscape and the redwood architecture.

Ultimately, these transformations create a building with an informed sensibility of continuity and extension that reaches beyond its walls. Spaces flow easily into each other, the surrounding landscape is made integral to the design rather than peripheral and the building sits within the landscape, rather than on it.

1   The redwood stair tower is a prominent feature
2   Horizontal and vertical planes intersect on the eastern façade
3   Clerestory windows flood the expanded foyer with light

1

2

3

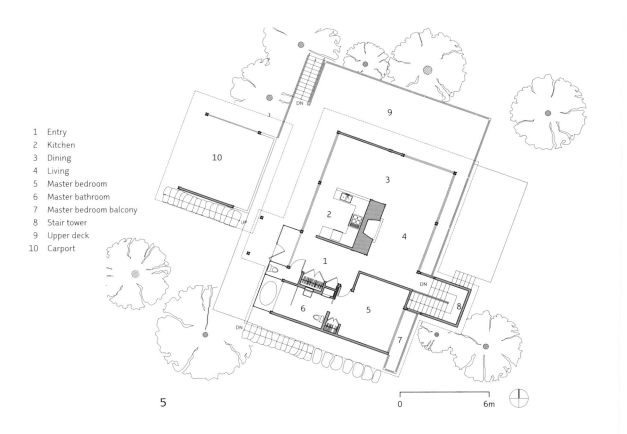

1   Entry
2   Kitchen
3   Dining
4   Living
5   Master bedroom
6   Master bathroom
7   Master bedroom balcony
8   Stair tower
9   Upper deck
10   Carport

0   6m

5

4

4   *The Sunshine Canyon House as seen from a distance*

5   *Upper floor plan*

6   *A horizontal wood screen creates patterns of light and shadow*

7   *Wide open interiors have unobstructed views of the countryside*

8   *The stair tower provides a light-filled transition between floors*

9   *Glass tile contrasts with the cleft slate flooring in the master bathroom*

Photography: Jonathan Schloss / Architect

6

8

7

9

TAN SHAW RESIDENCE

DELAWARE, PENNSYLVANIA, USA

SPACE4A

A professional couple working in New York City was looking to buy a weekend house in Pennsylvania close to the Delaware River. They were interested in a modern structure - a rare find in that region. After a long search they came across a residence that was originally built in the late 1960s in the shape of an arch. A previous owner had performed an unfortunate renovation eliminating large openings and replacing them with a rustic stucco façade with punched windows and a stone base. The client saw the potential for this unique structure - with its back built into a hill and a large roof overhang to the west - to open up to the surrounding landscape. Only trees surround the house and there are no neighbours in sight.

Space4a (partner in charge: Thomas Warnke) was hired to work on the re-design of the residence. The project team's main goals were to bring the house back to its original feel and to emphasise the original concept by maximising the amount of glazing and introducing a continuous polished-concrete floor running from inside to outside, strengthening the house's relationship with the landscape.

All interior partitions were removed and a plan developed with two guest bedrooms, one guest bathroom, a master bedroom suite and an open area with kitchen, dining and living spaces. The new partitions relate to the new 'storefront' system to which they are only connected by glass fins.

Entry to the house is via the dining area; to the left is the kitchen with white lacquered cabinets and black Corian counters; to the right is the open living room, which features a curved stone wall with a fireplace cut into it.

A corridor along the back wall leads to the guest area; the curve is highlighted by an indirect lighting feature at the ceiling. At night the building glows, becoming transparent due to a continuous line of strip lights along the curved 'storefront' system.

1

1 Dining area
2 Kitchen
3 Living area
4 Master bedroom
5 Master bathroom
6 Closet
7 Mechanical
8 Guest bedroom
9 Guest bathroom
10 Covered patio

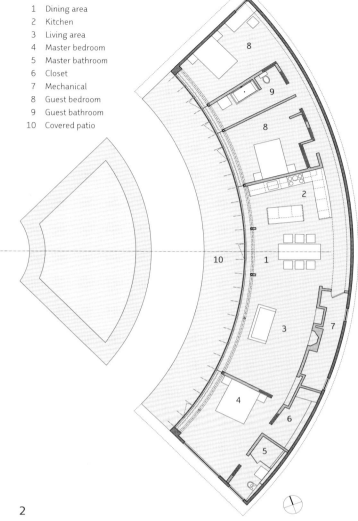

1 The building glows at night
2 Floor plan
3 Southeast view
4 Living room
5 Kitchen

Photography: Thomas Warnke

TICINO HOUSE

TICINO, SWITZERLAND

DAVIDE MACULLO ARCHITETTO

Located in one of sunniest areas of southern Switzerland, this house rises on a site once inhabited by old rural buildings. The structure's four solid volumes stand on the natural slope of the land, surrounded by nature. They follow the edges of the original building site and each has a carved roof reminiscent of those of the site's original buildings.

The landscape appears to flow through these volumes as if they are a continuation of the green environment. The cave-like entrance, surrounded by lawn, enhances this effect. The plan follows the contours of slope in an organic and fluent sequence of spaces that relate to each other and stretch outside. This typology offers an alternative to the ubiquitous box-shaped construction so prevalent on these hills, which are becoming increasingly urbanised – their unique qualities spoiled by aggressive building without respect to the environment.

The entire house has been built using eco-friendly construction materials such as Steko wooden blocks for the walls, TECU Classic and TECU Net for cladding, natural wood for flooring and gypsum board for the ceiling. The Steko system, utilised also for the internal partitions, is fully recyclable and reduces the time spent on site, with a corresponding reduction in noise, dust, site traffic and other environmental nuisances. The external skin is made of a copper screen, another natural and fully recyclable building material that protects the wooden internal envelope from overheating. In the House in Ticino, all these features combine with a high standard of living to define a new concept of comfort.

This project won the 2007 International TECU Award for the use of copper in architecture.

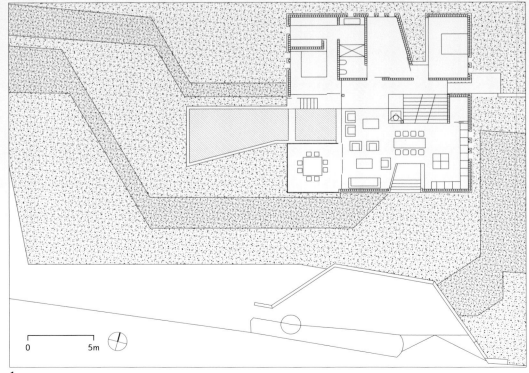

0   5m

1

2

4

3

5

1   Floor plan
2   View from east
3   View from west
4   Balustrade detail
5   TECU net screen detail

Photography: Enrico Cano

TREE HOUSE

WILMINGTON, DELAWARE, USA

SANDER ARCHITECTS

The Tree House sits on a wooded site surrounded by century-old trees and a seasonal stream. As a result of the site's vulnerability to flooding, the buildable area is quite small. The combination of the constraints of the 100-year floodplain on the building pad and the decision to preserve all the trees onsite led to the vertical form of the house. This form allows the house to sit within the trees with marvellous views of the canopy from the two upper floors.

Horizontal windows encircle the house and provide select views of the landscape. In contrast to these small views, a great wrapping window in the double-height living room provides a dominant diagonal focus for the house, and provides dramatic views into the deep woods.

The main living area is on the second level, while the main bedroom and ensuite bathroom occupy the entire third level. These raised spaces afford the feeling of being part of the canopy itself. Other useful spaces include a spare bedroom at the garage level and a study on the second floor.

The inside stairs were also designed by Sander Architects and fabricated at the performance stage shop where the owner works. They are made of 127-millimetre aluminium plate, with two treads in each unit. They bring a sculptural element to the dramatic living room and provide a counterpoint to the double-height fireplace wall clad with dark lavender slate.

Two exterior stairs provide access to the house. A front entrance stair, cantilevered out from the façade, enters through a trio of trees. This stair has bar-grate steps that provide a view of the stream below and also discourage snow build-up.

On the east façade, a spiral stair wraps from the ground level up to the roof deck, which doubles as an outdoor living space for tree-top entertaining.

1 South façade with view of the entrance stair from the streambed

2 View of entrance through trees

3 East façade with spiral staircase to rooftop

1

2

3

4   *Upper level plan*

5   *Main floor plan*

6   *Entrance stair with bar-grate treads and deck*

7   *Living room and view through surrounding trees*

8   *Aluminium staircase from living room to upper level*

9   *Living room with slate-clad fireplace*

Photography: © Sharon Risedorph of Sharon Risedorph Photography

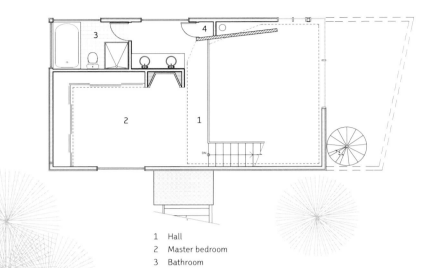

1   Hall
2   Master bedroom
3   Bathroom
4   Linen

4

1   Office
2   Kitchen
3   Pantry
4   Bathroom
5   Living room
6   Closet

0   2m

5

6

7

8

9

TWO WOLVES RESIDENCE

TETON COUNTY, WYOMING, USA

DUBBE-MOULDER ARCHITECTS

A picturesque, ski-in/ski-out private residence, Two Wolves is located at the base of the Jackson Hole Mountain Resort in Teton County, Wyoming. In collaboration with the owners, Dubbe-Moulder Architects designed a residence with a quiet presence that is integrated with the outdoors and epitomises the winter country home. A steep treed site created a dramatic backdrop and a platform for the residence to meld into the landscape.

A mix of details, texture and materials creates a visually appealing composition of regional materials on the façade. Combinations of vertical shiplap, horizontal plank and chink, horizontal bevelled siding, large plate glass windows, smooth and rough tile, excavated boulders and dry-stacked Montana stone were used to break up the faces. Outdoor living spaces surround the residence and extend the overall living space of the property. In addition to private balconies and public terraces, an outdoor spa offers a place to relax and enjoy the mountain views. Direct from the mountain, weary skiers are welcomed by a heated patio, a jetted hot tub and a gas fire.

Intended to surprise visitors moving through the home, the split-level entry relieves guests from travelling a full flight of stairs to get to the main level or to the basement. It redirects their interest to the curved staircase flanking the entryway, which in turn sparks intrigue about what lies at each end. The stairs lead to the main level where it is possible to see through almost the entire house. An open floor plan for living, dining and kitchen achieves the owners' vision of being able to comfortably entertain both small and large groups. The flexible, open space amplifies the indoor-outdoor relationship.

To define functional areas, ceiling beams and wall treatments create boundaries while retaining an open feeling. Two glass hallways extend from either side of the kitchen, drawing visitors through to discover private spaces. The suites in these spaces are well appointed and have a fireplace, private bath, sitting area and a balcony or patio. From the kitchen, the curved staircase winds up to a small loft, with an office and private balcony. The lower level to the left of the entry leads to the fireside games room, which includes an entertainment centre, a pool table and two guest suites. This wing has everything required for an enjoyable evening after skiing.

1   A grand entry welcomes guests to this ski-in/ski-out residence
2   Each bedroom suite has a private balcony
3   A view showing the house set into the mountainside
4   Surrounded by the forest, the terrace, with its hot tub and fireplace, provides memorable entertaining experiences

1

3

4

2

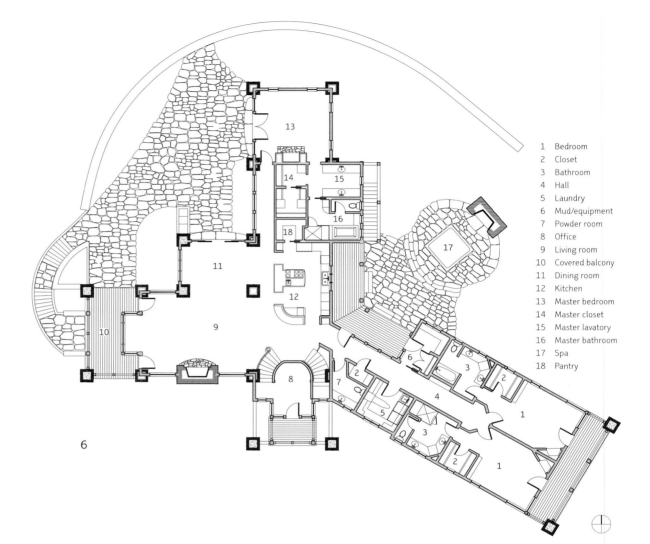

5   Master bedroom suite leading to outdoor terrace

6   Floor plan

7   Lower-level game and entertainment room

8   Ample glass allows the living room to have an outdoor
    experience

9   The open plan allows for living, dining and kitchen to
    maximise entertaining options

10 Living room

Photography: David Stubbs Photography

6

1	Bedroom
2	Closet
3	Bathroom
4	Hall
5	Laundry
6	Mud/equipment
7	Powder room
8	Office
9	Living room
10	Covered balcony
11	Dining room
12	Kitchen
13	Master bedroom
14	Master closet
15	Master lavatory
16	Master bathroom
17	Spa
18	Pantry

5

7

VILLA BLOCH-PASCHE

LAUSANNE, SWITZERLAND

**DL-A, DESIGN LAB-ARCHITECTURE SA
PATRICK DEVANTHÉRY & INÈS LAMUNIÈRE**

The Villa Bloch-Pasche is sited on the shore of Lake Lausanne in Switzerland. It is an ensemble made of a massive concrete block, hollowed out here and there to create loggias, terraces, a patio and a water basin.

The coloured cement layers without any joints and the larch-framed, flush-fitting window openings emphasise the notion of solidity and angularity of the shape – just like a sculpted piece of stone.

A large open space, oriented towards the lake, offers space for family life on the first floor. On the second floor, however, the individual rooms are differently proportioned, functionally interlaced and offer privacy and intimacy. The attic floor leans over the lake. The basement, on the other hand, has its own lookout that literally drills into the water. The Villa Bloch-Pasche has one form, but many atmospheres.

1

2

4

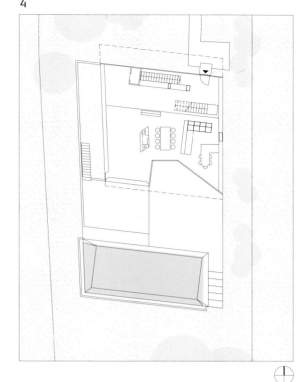

3

5

1   *The Villa: a massive concrete block in front of the lake*

2   *Spaces for daily family life*

3   *Dining room*

4   *First floor plan*

5   *The attic floor leans over the lake*

Photography: Fausto Pluchinotta, Geneva

VILLA D

STOCKHOLM, SWEDEN

RAHEL BELATCHEW ARKITEKTUR

Villa D is situated southeast of Stockholm on a steep and rocky site that overlooks a beautiful landscape. Two main criteria had to be considered in the design phase: the owners' wish to access the highest point of the site and their aim to limit the amount of excavation required.

RB Arkitektur designed a clearly defined volume that shoots out from the rock, creating a dramatic effect worthy of the site. The result is a long rectangular-shaped plan that is integrated into the rock on one end and cantilevered with an inclined gable on the other. In order to fulfil the owners' requirement of accessing the site's highest point, the living room, dining and kitchen areas are located on the first floor with access to large terraces, while bedrooms are positioned on the ground floor. A skylight stands above the staircase, making the access to the first floor bright and inviting.

While the building has a dramatic two-storey front façade, its rear face presents a discreet single storey turned towards a dense forest. The building is a combined timber-and-steel construction with façades clad in wood panels. The panels have been stained grey as a way of borrowing the colours of the surrounding nature.

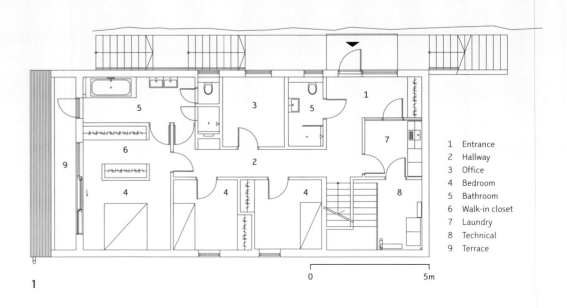

1   Entrance
2   Hallway
3   Office
4   Bedroom
5   Bathroom
6   Walk-in closet
7   Laundry
8   Technical
9   Terrace

0   5m

1

1   Ground floor plan
2   Front façade
3   Rear façade
4   Terrace facing the forest
5   Terrace on the first floor
6   Living room on the first floor

Photography: Rahel Belatchew Arkitektur

VILLA 'UNDER' EXTENSION

BLED, SLOVENIA

OFIS ARHITEKTI

This project involved the extension of a 19th-century villa located in a beautiful alpine resort adjacent to Lake Bled. Both the original villa and its surrounding landscape are strictly protected by Slovenia's National Heritage regulations. The client's primary request was for the main living area to be twice the size of the old existing villa. Additionally, most of the spaces were required to face the lake. The architect's main challenge was incorporating the new 700-square-metre addition while respecting all the regulations the villa and the surrounding landscape were subject to. Ofis Arhitekti's solution placed the new spaces beneath the ground floor of the existing villa.

The extension forms a rounded base, or 'pillow' beneath the house. Viewed from across the lake, the pillow blurs with its surroundings as it is integrated into the landscape with a green roof. The extension's elevation is glazed and overlooks the lake. The floor plan is organised in levels according to the outside landscape (plus or minus 50 centimetres) and the top of the pillow becomes a terrace and garden for the upper floor where the children's area is located.

The main living spaces (the ancillary kitchen, dining area, TV area, music space with fireplace, a library and work space) are all included in the new extension. Everyday service areas such as wardrobes, the main kitchen and the guest bathroom are located behind the walls of the original villa's cellar. Garages and storage/workshop spaces are also hidden in this volume. The original villa becomes a private rest area, with the children's space on the first floor and the parents' space on the top.

Entry is gained from the courtyard, which is displaced from the house's central axis. Across the curved ramp and beneath the staircase, a three-storey hall opens up to form the heart of the original villa, while the visual axis of the lake draws visitors into the new living area.

A curved stair defines and connects the old and the new, and functions as the main communications core in the house. All rooms and open spaces open onto the staircase and communicate with the main lobby.

Opposite   View from living area

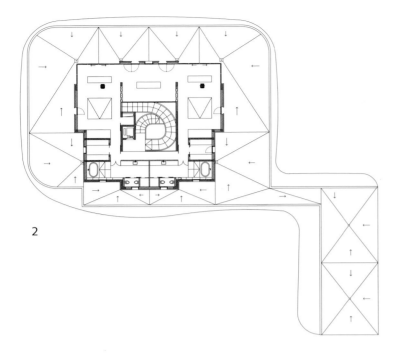

2

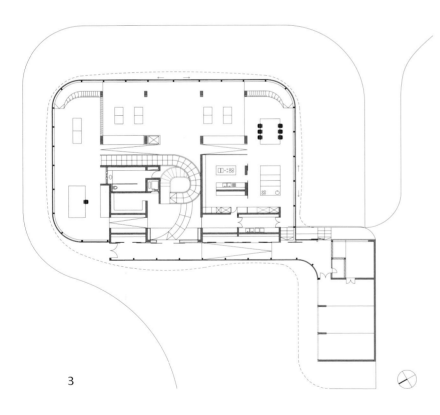

3

4

2 *Upper level floor plan*
3 *Lower level floor plan*
4 *Entrance courtyard*
5 *Under the communication void*
6 *Living area*

Photography: Tomaz Gregoric

5

6

THE VINTAGE

ROTHBURY, NEW SOUTH WALES, AUSTRALIA

SUTERS ARCHITECTS

The Vintage is a family home, an entertainment space, a lifestyle residence and a holiday house – all at the same address. It was the result of a restricted design competition in which eight architects were invited to propose designs for two homes each. The architects were required to present their schemes to the client and their competitors in a workshop environment. Three homes were chosen from three architects and two have now been built, including Suters' The Vintage.

The Vintage was designed to accommodate a number of variations including expansion to provide additional rooms or enlarge living spaces, different roof shapes (gable, curved or long skillion) and split levels for sloping sites. The client constructed the loft version, which provides an upper-level multipurpose space and includes a carport and golf buggy parking. The house has three bedrooms, two bathrooms and living, dining and kitchen spaces on an open floor plate with an attached screened indoor–outdoor space.

Designed to take advantage of its rural golf-course setting, The Vintage enjoys vistas of the course both within and through the building. It is a generally lightweight construction clad in vertical radial-sawn boarding with a metal roof. Detail elements including timber screens, a timber-and-steel pergola and a covered walkway assist the 'floating' aspect of the residence and yet, where appropriate, anchor the building to the ground. A coloured masonry-block entry wall acts as a spine that links the road to the golf course along the building length and directs pedestrian visitors to the entry. A raised terrace adjacent to the screened entertainment area provides external open space at the internal living level with access to the courtyard through large sliding doors.

The Vintage is a simple building structure that is constructed from honest building materials and formed with strong, uncomplicated detailing while responding to its bushland location.

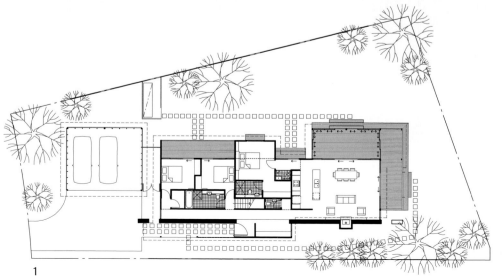

1

1   Floor plan
2   External view through bushland
3   Living area opening onto deck
4   Driveway arrival
5   Living room and fireplace
6   Living area opening onto deck

Photography: Rob Reichenfeld

THE VINTRY

POKOLBIN, NEW SOUTH WALES, AUSTRALIA

SUTERS ARCHITECTS

The Vintry is a country holiday house nestled against a backdrop of the Brokenback Ranges in Hunter Valley wine country. It enjoys a rural setting with an emphasis on lifestyle, relaxation and entertaining.

Located on a small vineyard, the house's simple linear form and outward orientation are designed to take advantage of the site. The masonry wall grounds the building, creating a spine and setting up an axis towards the vineyards and the Brokenback Ranges. Lightweight boxes are hung off either side allowing the house to float above the surrounding landscape and letting the shape of the land predominate.

The client's brief was for a luxury four-bedroom house with an emphasis on entertaining. The resulting house has three primary zones: the main entertaining area that enjoys the maximum impact of the view, a main bedroom wing that affords both privacy and outlook for the owner and a third zone containing the three guest bedrooms, each with their own bathroom and deck. A downstairs cellar allows the owners to indulge their love of wine. The main skillion roof unites the building and echoes the language of the local rural sheds, while the timber boxes, which will grey with time, add a modern slant.

The structure is essentially a masonry blade wall, steel frame and timber infill. The materials used were raw, enabling them to weather into a patina that would eventually allow the house to blend with the surrounding landscape. The interior floors are timber and walls are painted plasterboard or block. The cellar was left as raw concrete in keeping with its basement character. Overall, the house will require minimal maintenance – a useful feature in a holiday residence.

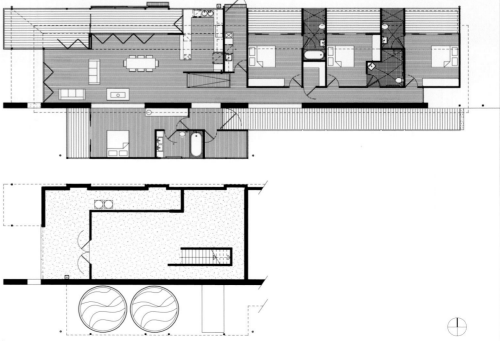

1

2

3

4

5

1   Floor plans
2   Interior gangway/bridge
3   Loggia with view to the Brokenback Ranges
4   Interior living space
5   Interior view along spine wall through clerestory corridor

Photography: Tyrone Branigan

WALTL RESIDENCE

MINDELHEIM, GERMANY

MCCLEAN DESIGN

This house is located in a traditional Bavarian village with a beautiful view over the fields towards the Alps. The site abuts an agricultural area that will function as a garden for the house. The village's design guidelines dictate that all local houses' upper levels must have vertical walls no higher than a metre and incorporate pitched roofs into their design. The Waltl Residence is a single-level home surrounding an internal courtyard, which provides a sheltered garden for outdoor living that extends the season for outdoor living.

The architect divided the house into two main blocks with vaulted ceilings and flat roofed sections, joining them around the courtyard. An office is placed as an object within the courtyard – a 'cockpit' from where much of the living space is visible, adjacent to the children's rooms. The primary living spaces are located at the rear where extensive glazing and operable doors connect the house to the surrounding landscape.

The courtyard is central to the play of light throughout the house and resonates particularly with one of the owners, as it is a common typology in her native country, Chile. The architect and owners were pleasantly surprised when the house received much support throughout the planning process. In such traditional villages, homes are often built in a certain way and materials are strictly limited in order to preserve a unified appearance. In this case, the Mindelheim City Council was open to a more contemporary interpretation and the Waltl Residence is the striking result.

1 Entry
2 Laundry
3 Garage
4 Bedroom
5 Bathroom
6 Exercise room
7 Living room
8 Office
9 Courtyard
10 Dining room
11 Kitchen
12 Family room
13 Closet

1

1   Floor plan
2   Side view showing rustic barns in the landscape
3   Courtyard view
4   The kitchen was designed as a self-contained element within the larger loft-like space
5   Living room area and view to fields beyond
6   Dining area with courtyard behind

Photography: Bernhard Weber

2

5

3

4

6

WATERFALL BAY HOUSE

WATERFALL BAY, MARLBOROUGH SOUNDS,
NEW ZEALAND

PETE BOSSLEY ARCHITECTS

The Waterfall Bay House is set on a sliver of bank squeezed between the hillside and the sea, tucked behind existing beech and kanuka trees. The lower levels were cut into the bank to reduce the impact of the overall form. Arrival to the property is normally by sea to the jetty, so the double-height glazed stair space reflects the axis of the arrival sequence.

The living areas are in the western wing with the guest bedrooms below. The main bedroom is separated by a cranked and rising glazed bridge, under which the landscape flows. To suggest the peripatetic nature of the owner's lifestyle the bedroom is projected out towards the sea on irregularly raking timber legs, as though it has just arrived, or is just about to leave.

The house forms, clad in vertical cedar, are penetrated by a series of irregular openings, establishing a variety of relationships between the interior spaces and the water immediately below, the bay and the ridgelines. The floor level and orientation of the main bedroom were carefully manipulated to ensure visual and acoustic contact with the waterfall, as was the western deck.

In order to create a sense of comfort and to avoid a sense of brittle 'newness', wide floorboards that will quickly age are combined with a variety of plywood linings, demolition hardwood beams and columns and timber joinery. The house is inhabited by a very personal collection of fine, well-worn, mainly mid-20th-century furniture and light fittings.

Careful selection of materials and systems such as recycled bridge timber and solar panels and thorough control of solar gain and loss ensure an environmentally sensitive design. The extended design development process ensured the house and external spaces reflect the owner's refined rituals associated with growing vegetables, raising chickens, cooking, reading, relaxing and entertaining.

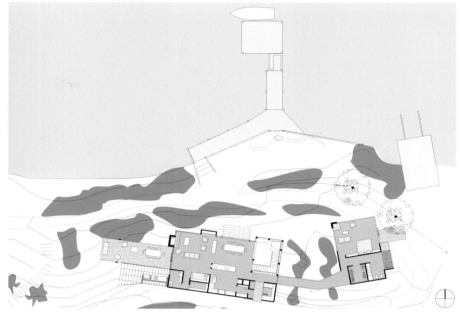

1   View from bay

2   View from bridge

3   From atrium towards main bedroom

4   Main bedroom with corner fireplace

5   Upper floor plan

6   Entry atrium with stairs

Photography: Paul McCredie (1,3,4); Kieran Scott (2,6)

WILKINSON HOUSE

PACIFIC NORTHWEST, USA

ROBERT OSHATZ

The Wilkinson House is an example of modern architecture at peace with its surroundings. It was designed so that the main level of the house sits amid the tree canopy on the steep site. Glass walls allow abundant natural lighting into the interior spaces and provide views to the surrounding canopy.

The exterior of the house consists of a series of horizontal layers featuring copper, cedar shingles and a copper roof. The entrance walkway passes through a small Japanese garden.

The interior has a spacious open plan with a variety of built-in furnishings, countertops and cabinets. The main living space consists of a single open area that includes a sitting area, a kitchen and dining area and a fireplace nook. The space then opens onto a large deck that cantilevers out among the trees. The house has a total floor space of 393 square metres: 234 square metres on the main level and 159 square metres on the lower level, which consist of three bedrooms and two-and-a-half bathrooms.

Natural materials including cedar shingles, wood trim, gypsum board, carpet, slate tile, granite tile and copper provide a variety of colours and textures to create a warm interior environment. The space seems to flow unobstructed between inside and out by continuing the interior materials through the glass walls and out to the exterior. Curves add a sense of tranquillity to the home: a series of curved, glue-laminated beams support the high ceiling, cedar shingles describe a series of organic curves and the glass-enclosed meditation room adjacent to the main space takes on a circular form.

As the owner is a lover of music, the architect carefully controlled the acoustics of the interior space and designed the volumes of the house to resonate with the flow of music.

1   *The glass walls of the main living space throw back
images of the forest canopy, helping to blend the building
into its environment*

1

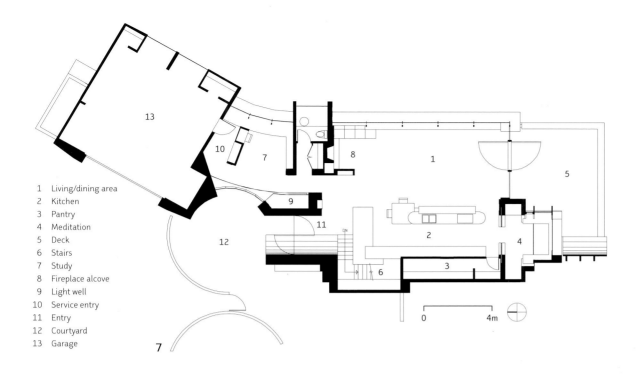

1 Living/dining area
2 Kitchen
3 Pantry
4 Meditation
5 Deck
6 Stairs
7 Study
8 Fireplace alcove
9 Light well
10 Service entry
11 Entry
12 Courtyard
13 Garage

6

8

2 The main living space extends over the lower floor out into the forest

3 From below the house appears to reach out into the forest canopy

4 A Japanese-style garden adorns the entry courtyard

5 The entry courtyard with Japanese garden from the front door

6 Curved glue-laminated beams flow over the main living space and out into the forest canopy

7 Floor plan

8 An open living space is divided into specific functions while maintaining its connection to the outdoors

9 A glass-enclosed mediation room extends out onto the deck and provides a serene space to read and relax

Photography: Cameron Neilson, Meredith Brower and Robert Oshatz

WINTER COTTAGE

BRIDGETOWN, WESTERN AUSTRALIA, AUSTRALIA

CHINDARSI ARCHITECTS

This cottage sits on a picturesque 9-hectare property that was once part of a former dairy farm, three hours by car south of Perth in Western Australia. Because of the owner's commitment to a sustainable future, the project was conceived around the principles of ecologically sustainable design and passive solar design. The idea was to design and build a small home for the owner and his visiting family while minimising the amount of material and embodied energy used. Simultaneously, the old family home in Perth was being demolished, and all the original jarrah doors, windows and eaves battens were salvaged and reused within the new context in some way. The home was created as a kit of parts primarily made in Perth and bolted together on site.

The home is a simple rectangular plan oriented 18 degrees off the east–west axis facing north. This minimises solar gain to the east and west faces of the home, and maximises solar gain from the north during winter. West-facing glass was all but eliminated, and the south-facing glass is protected from early and late summer sun through the use of the gabion rock screen wall. This steel-caged gabion stone wall functions as a 'filter', regulating light, air and temperature through the entry breezeway along the south side of the house. Reticulated dam water from the storage tank uphill trickles down this open mesh of rockwork, which acts like a 'Coolgardie safe' (an iconic Australian invention, which uses the principle of evaporation to keep food cool) by freshening the breezes through the house during the summer months via evaporative cooling. The home incorporates the use of a grid-connected photovoltaic array for the production of its own electricity, a solar hot water system, a waterless composting toilet, grey-water recycling through absorption trenching into the gardens below, a 100,000-litre rainwater tank for collecting drinking water and extensive sun shading. The bitterly cold winter nights are tempered by the home's small wood-fired 'Nectre' baker's oven. Extensive tree planting on the property since 1997 will eventually make the property self-sufficient for firewood.

1   Night view of eastern end of the cottage

1

2 *View along breezeway-link showing end of gabion wall*

3 *A lantern in the landscape*

4 *The undercroft guest area*

5 *View of dining room out towards the hills beyond*

6 *Main rooms folded open*

7 *View of kitchen towards translucent glazing of bathroom*

Photography: Robert Frith - Acorn Photo Agency

3

2

4

316

WOODEN HOUSE

CENTRAL BOHEMIA, CZECH REPUBLIC

SPORADICAL

The Wooden House is situated at the highest point of the northern slope of a former arboretum, with an area of 1.57 hectares. Both the location and size of the building were essentially formed by the structure of the original weekend house (part of the original foundation was used for the new house) and the close proximity of mature oak and fir trees. The brief was to create an economical residence with light and spacious rooms, closely linked to its natural surroundings.

The building is designed on three levels: an open residential ground floor, an enclosed bedroom floor and a rooftop terrace. The ground floor forms a single space with a central core, within which the kitchen facilities, technical area, storage spaces, staircase and fireplace are integrated. By using movable walls, the living area and kitchen can be separated from the southern corridor section, which can then be used as a winter garden. As a result of the positioning of the core, the outer walls can open onto a panoramic view of the surrounding landscape. The upper floor, by contrast, is the quiet and enclosed level of the house. It comprises a study, the parents' and children's bedrooms and a large bathroom. The bedrooms have narrow windows overlooking the garden and the large window above the bathtub frames a view of the treetops. From the bedroom, a 'secret' staircase leads along the façade to the rooftop terrace, which provides a pleasant situation for sitting and relaxing under the open sky.

The wooden frame construction allowed the exterior walls to be thinner and shortened the construction time. On the upper floor, the exterior walls are reinforced oriented strand board (OSB) slabs, which are part of the composition of the wall and simultaneously fulfil the function of vapour barriers. On the ground floor, the façade is formed from full-length sheets of insulating glass, anchored into the load-bearing pillars of the frame, along with small bottom-hung windows for ventilation and long French windows. The upper floor is clad with unplaned boards treated with protective varnish.

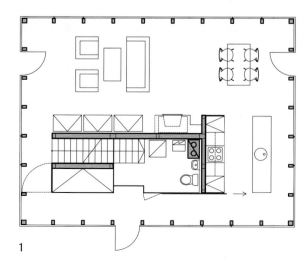

1

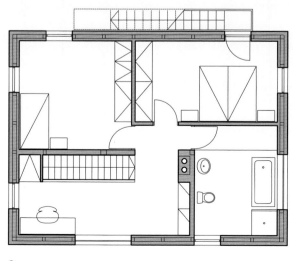

2

3

4

5

6

1   First floor plan
2   Second floor plan
3   Southeast perspective
4   Main living space

5   Ground floor illuminated at night
6   South-facing hallway

Photography: Jan Kuděj and Petr Sáva

WOOLSHED HOUSE

CARDRONA VALLEY, CENTRAL OTAGO, NEW ZEALAND

SALMOND ARCHITECTURE

This woolshed-inspired home, large enough for two families, is set on a rural property at the base of the Cardrona ski field. The simple forms, building proportions and materials allow the house to comfortably inhabit its rural setting.

The building echoes traditional farm structures in the Cardrona Valley – its simple gable and lean-to forms give it a timeless appearance.

The large north-facing central window with its sliding shutter evokes woolshed doors. Sliding doors open to the sun and views, providing an indoor–outdoor connection; shutters can be pulled across when the house is unoccupied. Corrugated steel cladding over a timber-frame structure contrasts with the timber windows, shutters and flooring, the recycled-hardwood interior doors and pergola and the timber trusses and timber sarking.

Heating and insulation are critical when the house is surrounded by snow. High levels of insulation in the roof, walls and floor ensure heat is retained in winter. The house is protected from the southerly wind by a buffer zone of spaces, including a wood store, entry porch, laundry and boot room.

Exposed framing, timber and corrugated steel sarking, a stone fireplace and timber floors continue the robust, rural feel inside the house. A stone fireplace dominates the southern end of the living area, and a wood-burning stove heats the rest of the living space. Under-floor heating warms the concrete floors of the bedrooms and bathrooms.

A vertical slot window and continuous skylight at the junction between the gable and lean-to roofs bring light and shafts of sun into the centre of the square plan. Four small windows reflect the internal layout of the bunk room, giving each occupant control of light and ventilation. The master bedroom upstairs has a view to the clock tower at the Cardrona ski field.

1   West wall showing bunkroom windows and woolshed form
2   North elevation with recycled-timber pergola and shutters closed
3   Ground floor plan
4   Kitchen with study above

Photography: Salmond Architecture

1

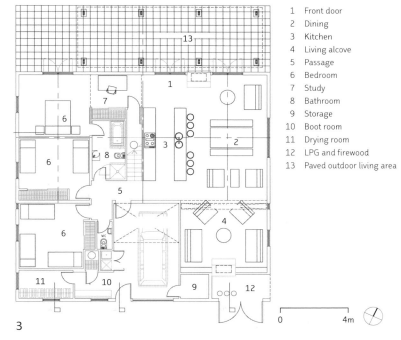

1	Front door
2	Dining
3	Kitchen
4	Living alcove
5	Passage
6	Bedroom
7	Study
8	Bathroom
9	Storage
10	Boot room
11	Drying room
12	LPG and firewood
13	Paved outdoor living area

3

0   4m

2

4

INDEX OF ARCHITECTS

Every effort has been made to trace the original source of copyright material contained in this book. The publishers would be pleased to hear from copyright holders to rectify any errors or omissions.

The information and illustrations in this publication have been prepared and supplied by the participants. While all reasonable efforts have been made to ensure accuracy, the publishers do not, under any circumstances, accept responsibility for errors, omissions and representations express or implied.